SING ME THE CREATION

by

Paul Matthews

A book of exercises, structured in such a way that both the skills and the imaginative faculties involved in creative writing can be developed.

Though intended for group work with adults, teachers of children will find many new ideas for the classroom, and individuals working alone will have no difficulty adapting the exercises to their situation.

HAWTHORN PRESS

Published by Hawthorn Press, 1 Lansdown Lane, Stroud, GL5 1BJ, U.K.
Copyright © 1994 Paul Matthews
Reprinted 1996

Paul Matthews is hereby identified as the author of this work in accordance with Section 77 of the Copyright, Designs and Patent Act, 1988. He asserts and gives notice of his moral right under the act.

Typeset by Saxon Graphics Ltd, Derby
Printed by Redwood Books Ltd, Trowbridge
Cover illustration: 'Adam naming the beasts' by William Blake, courtesy Glasgow Museums: The Stirling Maxwell Collection, Pollok House, Glasgow.

A catalogue recording for this book is available from the British Library.
ISBN 1 869 890 60 4

This book is dedicated to *Francis Edmunds* (founder of Emerson College) who gave me the opportunity, and to *Elizabeth Edmunds* who recognized the possibility.

My thanks go to the many students and colleagues who have worked with me over these years. Whether or not their words are included here, the warmth and inspiration that they brought is surely folded into these pages.

Thanks, also, to Mairead Porter for typing the manuscript. Much of the final shaping is due to her labour, skill and interest.

My wife, Margli, has been a constant source to test my truth upon, and I don't know how to begin to thank her for it.

Paul Matthews was a student at Sussex University, 1963-66. While living in Brighton he worked with the poet George Dowden and edited a poetry magazine, *Eleventh Finger*, with Paul Evans, taking particular interest in what was happening in American poetry. After University he became a student at Emerson College, preparing to be a teacher in Steiner (Waldorf) education. It was there that he met his wife, Margli. They have two daughters. After teaching children for a few years he returned to Emerson College as a teacher of Creative Writing and Gymnastics, two seemingly divergent activities which gradually came together in the creation of this book. Besides teaching at Emerson he has been an instructor in the British School of Bothmer Gymnastics, and has travelled widely in the U.K., Germany, U.S.A., Australia and New Zealand, giving workshops in writing and readings of his own poetry. Currently available from the author is, *The Ground that Love Seeks* (Five Seasons Press). His overriding concern is for the role of poetry as a community-making activity, and as a means of schooling the imagination. At present he is offering a longer Course in Creative Writing at Emerson College, and is teaching in the School of Storytelling. He is available to give workshops based upon the contents of this book.

CONTENTS

A WELCOME

To this hearth which is a heart, welcome.
Welcome to our hearts. Welcome to our breath
        seeking to be song.

May those without a place tonight
        find welcome here.

May those without a tongue be brought to utterance.

Welcome to the stone that has no mouth to cry with.

Welcome to the leaf that trembles on the edge
        of speaking.

Welcome to the owl's high lonely questioning.

May our ears catch answers.

May the Word which hovers above our heads
        find hospitality.

May the song which crosses
between the living and the dead
be part of what we sing.

Welcome to the fabulous Names of things.

Foreword

Paul Matthews' *Sing Me The Creation* stands as probably the most
unusual guidebook for creative writing in the world. Some eighteen
years ago, when I was a university professor teaching in a program in
depth psychology and literature, I had the privilege of working with
Caroline Gordon. She was an accomplished novelist, in the tradition of
the great writers of the American South, such as William Faulkner and
Eudora Welty, and was also intimately involved in the movement
known as the New Criticism, with significant writers such as John
Crowe Ransom. Miss Gordon taught creative writing. Through her I
learned that it was not possible to get very far by approaching writing
through the kinds of technical manuals in vogue. Her approach was to
immerse students in the great literature of the world. Her notion was
that it was more important to develop imagination than to work at
writing skills. She was astute enough to know that imagination was not
a subjective reality, and that great literature changes the world and
could therefore change potential writers as well. I always felt that she
had solved half of the problem of learning to write. Now, after eighteen
years of waiting, I think that Paul Matthews has solved the other half.

In this book, Paul Matthews provides an effective guide into the
imagination of the word. Further, his approach to the word is
somewhat akin to that of Owen Barfield: he has found a way to enter
into the word that is at the same time a gateway into an imagination of
the soul of the world.

Technical approaches to writing do not work because they are
infected with the great disease of language, nominalism. Nominalism
sees the word as no more than an instrument, empty of any substance
of its own, language as a mere device for bringing the mind out into the
open. To understand what constitutes a paragraph, a sentence, a
metaphor, a simile, preposition, synonym, antonym can be seen as

nothing more than a technology of nominalism. This approach to the word has been with us since the seventeenth century and can be traced to Marin Mersenne. Mersenne carried on a thirty-years intellectual war, taking the side of rationalism against imagination. He took metaphorical statements at their literal level and tried to show that imagination-imbued language was nonsense. For example, he posed questions such as "How high is Jacob's ladder?" Such a question cannot be answered, for "Jacob's ladder" is imaginative rather than scientific language. Through the centuries this scientific view of language has taken hold; we are all infected with it. In the domain of the literary arts, the final result of nominalism is that the world of fiction is reduced to entertainment, reading a form of self-indulgence, words a vehicle for conveying untruth, writing only a means of expressing subjective imagination that has nothing to do with the 'real' world.

In the past decade or so, another approach to creative writing has sprung up. Instead of the deadly approach to the technology of language, aspiring writers are now doing inner visualization work, paying attention to dream images, shifting attention to the inner world. The intention here is to learn how to stay close to the image, and to write directly out of the inner experience of image. Such psychological approaches to creative writing put the emphasis on creative rather than the act of writing. No doubt this shift is due to a popularizing of Jung's psychology. I suspect that writers enjoy these kinds of workshops, not recognizing that subjective approaches to imagination cannot heal the illness of the word; it is a little like seeking a cure for cancer by going to the movies.

My friend and colleague, James Hillman, had written as early as the 1970s that in the field of language what is needed is a new *angelology* of words so that we may once again have faith in them. Angel means "emissary", "message-bearer", and that is exactly the kind of renewal of the word we find here in this wonderful book. Hillman is not suggesting that words bring to us the messages of the angelic world, but that words themselves are angel worlds. Seeing words as angels, as independent carriers of soul, and soul as referring to the inner quality of all things, not simply to subjective experience, saves us from the suffocating thought that speech is no more than the utterance of personal opinions. Hillman's proposal has the capacity to alter completely our now unconscious habit of using words thoughtlessly. But, how to go about inhabiting words as holy messengers, the actual task of doing the necessary work, that is found here in *Sing Me The Creation*.

Because the word as angel of the soul has atrophied to an alarming extent, the sclerotic body of language has to be taken out of five centuries of imprisonment and given healthy exercise. This book is filled with exercises which can be seen as homeopathic remedies. If the word is ill then it is the word that can heal; that is a homeopathic principle. Technical exercises, which are something completely different than what is found in this *materia medica* of the word, exercise only the physical, literal body of language. Such exercise may build muscle, but leave the soul untouched and sick. Exercises of the inner imaginary life may enrich fantasy, but do not strengthen the speech organs, and soul is set adrift without a body. Another aspect of approaching healing homeopathically is that the forces of healing are not brought in from the outside but come through the development of one's own inner forces. Mr. Matthews does not do the work for us; he only indicates a healthy way of working.

The exercises recommended herein have an additional dimension that goes even further than homeopathic remedies. The healing of the word is not only based on the principle that like cures like. The truly great contribution of this book is to be found in its putting forth the basic truth that the word is the whole of the universe, the Logos. Here homeopathy, which is a strictly empirical approach to healing, is taken up and fulfilled by anthroposophical remedies. The remedies of anthroposophic medicine, while also homeopathic, are based on knowledge of the correspondences between the body, soul, and spirit of the individual with the rhythms of the creating powers of the universe. Thus, the exercises in this book are more than empirically based experiments that have been found to work based upon other than mechanistic assumptions. Each set of exercises also embodies one of the qualities of the creating elements of the world – Earth, Water, Air, and Fire. The elements are not material substances as we have now come to think of them but are pure qualities of creative activity unifying both inner soul and outer reality. Further, this arrangement is far more than a scheme oriented toward bringing order to the way one goes about working anew with language. The work Mr. Matthews invites the reader to participate in is none less than renewing the universe through re-enlivening the word.

The scope of this book really takes it altogether out of the realm of a self-help instruction manual for writers. As it begins to dawn on the reader that the approach of this work concerns healing the world through healing the word, what first was perhaps seen as an innovative way of teaching creative writing now appears as an essential discipline of world renewal. This discipline fosters interiority of word and world, the co-penetration of one with the other. Thus, this is a book of spiritual practices, taken out of the realm of pious religiosity that has nothing to do with the actual world within which we live and properly placed within the practical dimensions of everyday life.

Anyone serious about the craft of writing is bound to feel sheer joy and delight that someone has finally acknowledged that writing is not a lonely, private endeavour that some few people seem to have to do, not knowing exactly why. In effect, Paul Matthews is saying that writing is world work, and those engaged in such work are an invisible community doing the most practical work imaginable. And anyone serious about spiritual practice will be equally delighted to find that they are part of this same invisible community, silently working toward world renewal. It is not at all accidental, then, that most of the exercises in this book are best carried out in a communal setting. Further, communal here means more than a group of people all doing the same thing. These exercises, like the creating powers of the universe itself, do not take place by each individual privately following instructions while happening to be in the same room with others. The exercises are based on the principle that the part is equal to the whole. Thus, the individuality of those doing these exercises together is not annihilated for the benefit of the whole, as often happens when activities are put forth as communal. Rather, true individuality is to be found in the fact that we are each the whole of the universe, but at the same time, this wholeness needs the equal wholeness of other individualities in order to be rightly expressed.

I do not want, by trying to point out the tremendous significance of this book, to imply that this work is destined to be of interest primarily to the serious-minded, the esotericists, the occultists, the metaphysicians of the world. Quite the contrary. While I do want to emphasize that learning the skills of writing as put forth here is in fact learning the skills of living in a new way that is desperately needed, perhaps the ultimate value of this book is that it is **great fun**. The exercises are humorous, delightful, surprising. The vision of this work is comic, which does not mean just funny, but rather corresponds to the creative genre of the universe in terms of its destiny rather than its origins. My most significant teacher, Dr. Louise Cowan, a noted literary critic, has a wonderful view of the world as epic, tragic, lyric, and comic. All of the great literature of the world, it seems, falls into one of these domains, with a few transitional forms that bridge between. The epic has to do with the forming of the earthly world in conjunction with the powers of the gods. The tragic vision has to do with the necessary creative mistake of the individual hero trying to make a single view stand in for the whole. The lyric vision is a recovery of the whole, but as existing within the individual soul. The comic vision is the restoration of the whole, and is characterized as a marriage between the human and the divine. The restoration is, of course, always accompanied with laughter and mirth because this union is inexplicable to the rational mind. Great effort may be put into trying to find wholeness, but in the end, it is a matter of grace as much as human effort. The exercises in this book are certainly hard work. But, in doing them, there is always the moment in which laughter intrudes, an indication that the angels of words have indeed been invited back to inhabit language. The perceptible movement of their wings, I suspect, tickles us.

When a rare book such as this is published, one always wonders where it will be put on the shelves of bookstores. It belongs in the self-help section. It also belongs in the section on theology and religion, psychology, spirituality, hermeticism, literature, poetry, art, and humour. In truth, it does not matter where this book is shelved as it is one of those works which will locate its readers rather than readers locating it. This book, I predict, will more or less find its own way into the world, for after all, it has wings.

Robert Sardello, Ph.D.
Author of *Facing the World With Soul*
and *Love and the Soul*

One

A Personal Introduction

How this book came to be written

At the age of 17, out of the shock of finding my awakening inner life echoed in the work of the English Romantic poets, I began to write my own poetry. Right from the start I was deeply interested in the creative sources of my art, and it seemed natural after that first adolescent discovery to take up the study of English literature at university. I did. And I was disappointed.

Looking back now it is clear that the studies there were based on a conscious separation between the content of a text studied and the student's personal and creative life. A friend in the Theology department, for instance, received one of her more impassioned essays back with the comment, 'You are not here to engage in a personal search.' At the time such attitudes enraged me, for that, precisely, was the search I was engaged in. Writing for me was a path of inner transformation as well as a potential work in the world. Not that I regret those years. My tutors were honest in the stance they took, testing the too easy Romanticism of my youth, and I am thankful to them for showing me the shape of the problem; but I had to turn elsewhere to find the teachers who could help me resolve it.

First there was George Dowden (an American poet long resident in England) – I must acknowledge him. He represented quite the other pole to the 'word-poetry' of my University studies. I have wrestled with him a great deal since about whether 'word-poetry' and 'life-poetry' are necessarily exclusive of each other; but I am grateful to him for being a living example of what a teacher of writing might be, helping me with my craft and enlarging my vision of what is happening in 20th century literature. Through him I began to feel myself part of a community of young writers, linked through a network of small magazines, including 'Eleventh Finger' which I edited with Paul Evans. That was a time (late 1960s) of much experimentation in literary forms, and of a renewed spirit of Romanticism, kindled through contact with figures such as Allen Ginsberg and Denise Levertov in America. This period culminated for me in the discovery of the San Francisco poet, Robert Duncan. He has been a major inspiration for my life and work, teaching me, above all, that there is life in language and that, conversely, all the seemingly random happenings of our lives speak truly of who we are.

Then, at the age of 28, I found myself teaching creative writing and gymnastics at Emerson College in Sussex, a training centre based on

'Christ as Anthropos', from Bartholomaeus Angelicus, Le Proprietaire des Choses, Trustees of British Museum.

the work of Rudolf Steiner (1861-1925). I must acknowledge him, too, for it is his vision which provides the context for what I have tried to bring together in this book. Much could be said about this extraordinary man, but it must suffice now to say that what attracted me most immediately to his work was the recognition that here (to use Owen Barfield's words) was a 'Romanticism come of age'. Not only did Steiner acknowledge (with John Keats) the truth of the Imagination; he explored ways in which this faculty could be developed as a mode of exact perception and applied in a holistic approach to practicalities such as farming, teaching, medicine, to name just a few. He spoke further about the faculties of Inspiration and Intuition – progressive steps towards bridging the gulf between 'self' and 'world'.

In this picture of the potentially free and creative human being I began to see how my old question concerning the split between objective study and personal search might be resolved. The modern critical mind, for example, enables us to analyse language into its operative parts – the facts of grammar. With a little exercise of the Imagination however (and without denying the 'facts') we can perceive that the laws of grammar are an outward manifestation of the laws at work in the human soul, and that the same 'Logos' is involved in the shaping of the world around us. The structure of this book and the writing exercises contained in it are the result of my working for many years as poet and teacher out of this essential insight.

N.B. In this book the word 'poetry' is used very broadly, describing a way of seeing and knowing the world, not just a way of writing about it. Such a 'poetry' can certainly find its way into prose forms as well as into verse, and these are included here as part of the work.

Renewing the Ancient Hearth

At the very beginning of English literature stand the words:

Sing me the Creation

or, in the Anglo-Saxon of the original, 'Sing me Frumsceaft'. They appear in the Venerable Bede's famous 7th century history of Caedmon, the first English poet that we know by name. One evening when Caedmon was feasting with his friends he saw the harp being passed towards him around the hearthfire and, feeling shy about his lack of skill in singing, he gave some excuse about having to look after the animals and slipped away. Out there in the barn he fell asleep, and in his dream an Angel came to him and said, *"Caedmon, sing me something."* He answered and said, "I cannot sing so I left the feasting and came here because I could not." He who spoke to him again said, "Nevertheless, you can sing to me." He said, "What shall I sing?" He said, "Sing me the Creation." It is a marvellous, two-fold commission, and central to the work of any poet –

> to praise the glory of the created world
> to care for the sources of creativity and Imagination.

Bede goes on to tell us that Caedmon composed in his sleep a hymn to the Creator [see *p. 183*] and that in the morning he knocked at the door of the nearby monastery to ask for help in writing it down. Later he himself joined the monastic community and became a composer of verses on Christian themes *–Like a clean animal he ruminated and converted all into the sweetest music.*[1]

I am in two minds about Caedmon. On the one hand he received this great commission from the Angel and passed it on to us. On the other, his act of breaking the tribal circle epitomizes a fundamental shift in Western culture, away from a community of language around the hearthfire towards the image we have of the lonely poet pouring a personal anguish upon the page, or of the professional writer intent upon fame and originality. Undoubtedly it was a necessity of the times; the tribal lore was bound to fall apart in the face of a Christianity which preached:

I am come to set a man at variance against his father, and the daughter against her mother, and the daughter-in-law against her mother-in-law. And a man's foes shall be they of their own household. He that loveth father or mother more than me is not worthy of me.[2]

(St. Matthew Ch. 10)

But today with equal necessity the urge arises for a renewal of that hearth, no longer through the blood-ties of the immediate 'kin', but in free companionship, whatever our sex, age, race, religion, culture or colour. This book, (though it clothes itself in the English tradition of my own upbringing), is dedicated to that ideal. Rather than trying to meet everyone on their own ground, I wish to acknowledge both the gifts and the limitations of my own sources, and to trust that those who have other cultural backgrounds will be inwardly free enough to transpose the content of this book into a mode suited to their own lives.

The Saxon poet, Widsith, wandering from hearth to hearth in the practice of his craft is described as unlocking his 'word-hoard', and no doubt helping others to unlock theirs.[3] His was neither a personal nor an original art in our modern sense, but a drawing upon the common heart and memory of the folk, speaking their Origins, their common story.

With the breakdown of established religion, however, and with the mixing of cultures in our times, it seems we have lost all sense of our common story. So if a group or class gathers intent upon writing and creating together (and this book assumes it) we must find some other starting point. W.B. Yeats expressed it very clearly when he said:

> ....*Now that my ladder's gone,*
> *I must lie down where all the ladders start,*
> *In the foul rag-and-bone shop of the heart.*[4]
> (from *The Circus Animals' Desertion*)

Maybe when we meet there seems to be nothing at all between us; yet if you give me your word I can reply with the next, collaborative, responding to questions asked, needs recognized, testing each other's immediate joys and fears in the writing. That is how I started my work as a poet-teacher – with nothing, almost, with simple human acts of language – till gradually I became aware that through a word or a sentence shared in writing we could move into the presence of a communion greater than anything I had intended. At such moments it was no longer a classroom with me, as teacher, at the centre. It became a 'circle of truth, poetry and love' in which we were all servants of the Word, the Logos, that is beyond any skill or genius that we might have in language.

Therefore, if I call this a 'sourcebook' I do not mean merely a textbook from which to learn competence in writing. I mean a book where exercises in the craft are also (if you will) inner exercises leading both to self-knowledge and to an understanding of the language that Nature is. And when I say 'a sourcebook for poets', I am referring to a possibility which dwells within us simply through the fact of our being human. My basic assumption throughout has been that each one of us has a unique voice which, despite all the inhibitions and thwartings that life brings, can receive permission to speak. It is fundamental to the work of a poet to make this possible, and the writing group (so long as it is free from competitive or commercial interests) can be the means of achieving it. Language comes alive between people.

Inhibitions

From childhood onwards we live with the insistence of parents and teachers, that language (and thence our thinking and feeling) should be brought within the civilized bounds of correct pronunciation and spelling, proper sentence structure, essays having a beginning, middle and end, and so on. We are taught to be truthful at all times and, of course, not silly or boastful. Perhaps the greatest inhibition of all is that language must be a tool for meaning – absolutely necessary, no doubt (and the laws of grammar are fundamental to this book), but taken to an extreme this insistence can crush all life and play out of the language, so that writing and speaking must always be the expression of what we know already, and not the result of listening, not the discovery of what moves here in the moment. Thus our word-hoard gradually gets locked up inside us, our true voice stifled; and when the burning Harp comes near us Caedmon's blush is on our faces.

Permissions

Therefore, at the outset of this work together, the following *poetic license* is granted:

1. You may break the rules of any exercise that is set here.
2. You may, when the need arises, use 'bad' English, begin in the middle, leave your work unfinished etc.
3. You may write in collaboration with your neighbour.
4. You may copy your neighbour's work.
5. You may be silly or meaningless. There is no need to be profound or literary. "Absolute rubbish" is permitted.
6. You may tell 'lies', and exaggerate.
7. You may speak to things and flowers and animals and strangers and to yourself. You may speak for them. You may speak to God.
8. You may be personal and 'subjective' and sentimental – a participator and exclaimer as well as the detached observer and reporter.
9. You may enjoy yourself.

Playing

The philosopher, the theologian, the scientist, the butcher, the baker, all have their tasks and truths to be rightfully serious about. But the poet? What does the poet have to deal with seriously unless it be the realm of play which of all realms seems the least to warrant it?

Friedrich Schiller (in his *Aesthetic Letters*)[5] expresses the view that for most of the time we are bound – either by the laws of logic, or by outer necessity. Only in play, he says, can we be free from them, or free to balance their one-sided tyrannies. 'Man is fully human only when he plays, and he only plays when he is human in the fullest sense of the word.' In an extension of the concept he then goes on to say that art too belongs to this realm of freedom, and by that definition poetry would be something very serious indeed – the enactment of our full humanity.

So if in the writing group we begin by playing together it need not be seen as a 'trivial' activity (though I have often heard the word); it offers the possibility of entering once again that state called childhood where, totally intent upon the act, we heal the division in our consciousness.

Writing can become very intense and inward at times, so play and laughter (as well as tears) are a vital part of any group work. This is gloriously expressed in the apocryphal 'Hymn of Jesus', where Christ, just before entering the very depth and seriousness of his Passion, says – 'I am the Word who did play all things and was not shamed at all.'[6]

How to use this book

You are welcome, of course, to use it as a source book for your private work in writing.

It is conceived, however, as a basis for group work – with adults primarily, but a resourceful teacher adapting and selecting would certainly find it invaluable in work with children.

However you use it, feel free to outleap the limits that the book-form necessarily imposes upon the content. I have tried to overcome this by the use of cross-references and repetition, but this really only points to the need for the group leader (if there is one) to be so familiar with the whole, and sure of his/her own resources, that relationships between sections can be made freely.

Suggestions for group practice

It is often helpful to kindle a sense for image, sound, rhythm through small, playful, collaborative exercises before moving into individual or more intensive work.

Read out in the group the pieces that you have written (but also respect silence). If writing with a partner, consider together what you have written before reading it out. Thus, we all become teachers, assessing ourselves and coming to our own questions rather than being judged by others.

Keep everything that is written, even 'mistakes', so that they can be referred to or read out on a later occasion. Whatever is written is, in fact, the shared substance of the group, the beginning of its 'common story'.

Use unlined paper. Poetry is a field of energy, and too many bars can imprison it.

If you are the teacher or group leader, write with your students. Try not to impose your style as a group expectation. You can learn too. Keep the exercises in the artistic realm. They may be psychologically healing, but that is better left unsaid.

The structure of this book

The structure (and central imagination) of this book is based on a fact of grammar – that there are four kinds of sentence:

Statement: Question: Exclamation: Command.

Everything that we say or write is bound to be one of these, or something recognizably in between. They can be characterized as follows:

STATEMENT: the act of naming, describing, defining the state or the truth of things.

QUESTION: language between you and me; the dialogue.

EXCLAMATION: where inner feeling comes directly to expression in language.

COMMAND: language as power and movement, directing will into the world.

Exhortations, such as 'God save the Queen', may somewhat elude these categories; yet this fourfoldness (as we shall see) is archetypal both to the created world, and to human activity. In mathematics we find it in the four principles of addition, subtraction, multiplication and division, which need to be thoroughly practised and understood before anything else is possible. It is the same with language, and on the basis of this fourfoldness the book has been divided into sections. But first we must consider the whole.

Hieronymus Bosch: The Prodigal Son.

Exercise 1
Approach this painting through each of these acts of language. In a group different people can be given different tasks:

Statement:

> *e.g. The sky is cloudy above, lightening a little as it reaches the horizon. On the left is a ramshackle house with a broken roof. The shutters are hanging from one nail, flapping against the windows. An old woman is peering into the yard. Hidden around the corner of the house a man is peeing. In the doorway stands a thin man trying to kiss the barmaid. On one side of the house hangs an Inn sign with a white swan depicted on it, while on the other side a caged Magpie is hanging.*

Question:

> *e.g. Why is the owl out in daylight? Why does this man wear unmatching shoes? What is in his basket? Does the Magpie in the cage know the Magpie at the gate? Why does the poor man turn his head? Does the woman in the window love him? Does the girl in the doorway really want to be kissed? Why is it so dark inside the house? Will the gate let this poor man through? Will the cow butt him? Why does the horizon pass right through his head?*

Exclamation:

> *e.g. How poor this man is! Such sad eyes! Yet he's wise, too! How I wish I could help him! He must be very hungry! What a strange man he is, though! Fancy having two hats! And unmatched shoes! Wise, yes! But he's a fool, too! What a stupid way to carry a basket!*

Command:

> *e.g. Come out of that tree, owl. Wind, stop blowing. Woman, stop looking. Come, Man, come and say goodbye to me. House, stop standing. Leave your cage, bird. Cap in my hand, show me the right way. Sing, Magpie, sing. Stop being so heavy, basket. Trees, greet me from afar. Landscape, don't remind me of my home so far away.*

Each of these four acts of language embodies a certain ideal. In practising them, therefore, we are exercising human virtues as well as sharpening the power of our word.

The Statement seeks to be true and clear at least and, lastly, to be wise.

The Question cannot be a question unless it is receptive. It springs out of inter-est. Questions that begin with, 'Wouldn't you agree that ....' are really statements in disguise.

The Exclamation seeks to be the full expression of what the heart holds. It strives for beauty.

The Command seeks to be effective in the world, powerful for the good.

The four temperaments

If the results of this first exercise are read out in the group it will quickly become clear that these four sentence types are also four different ways in which we relate to the world. The ancient world referred to this fourfoldness in our human nature as the four temperaments – Choleric, Sanguine, Phlegmatic and Melancholic – and Rudolf Steiner, in developing a form of education devoted to the unfolding of the child's creative potential, has made them new for our time.[7] As they are essential to an understanding of this book I will attempt briefly to describe them.

First, it needs to be said that 'temperament' does not refer to the deepest individuality of a person, but rather to the given instrument through which they express themselves in life. As such, it can be experienced as both a gift and a limitation. Ideally, the temperaments are balanced within the adult person, or a balance can be worked for, but before we can do so we need to recognize them in their extremity:

Choleric: These people have great strength of ego and a mind of their own. No sooner do they have an idea than they seek to transform it into action and, because obstacles do not deter them, they persevere until the task is accomplished. They are natural leaders, full of optimism, with their sights set on the future. On this account they can be over-impetuous, quick-tempered and aggressive, with little patience for others. They are easily recognized by their determined walk, prominent chin and often dark and challenging eyes.

Sanguine: These people have a great eagerness for life. Their attention is quickly aroused by a new idea, or by whatever butterfly happens to be fluttering past them; and so, just as easily, they lose interest again. This living always for the present can lead to a certain superficiality and unreliability; yet without their easy-going nature and infectious

liveliness the social life would be a dismal affair. They are often fair
with blue eyes, well-proportioned, moving gracefully and lightly upon
their toes.

Phlegmatic: These people carry with them a sense of inward harmony
and well-being, especially after meals. They are calm, patient, round,
self-contained – sometimes to the point of being cut off from their
surroundings and lazy in their dealings with life. At their best, though,
they can be faithful friends, great carers and nurturers, spreading a cosy
warmth around them. In their movements they are rather slow and
clumsy. They, too, live easily in what the present moment provides.

Melancholic: These people, though not heavily built, give the
impression of being weighed down by life. They are quiet and serious,
yet their keen observation of life gives them a telling sense of
humour. They are strongly drawn to the past, forever brooding upon
real or imagined problems. Knowing the pain of life they can show
much sympathy for the sufferings of others. Often they have strong
artistic gifts. They can be recognized by their measured steps and their
slight stoop as they walk.

Rudolf Steiner summarized their qualities in a diagram:

Melancholic
attention not easily aroused
strongly persevering

Phlegmatic   **Choleric**
attention least easily aroused   attention most easily aroused
least strongly persevering   most strongly persevering

Sanguine
attention easily aroused
little strength of perseverance

These temperaments are not often found in their pure form. The
Choleric, for instance, may well have traces of melancholy or
sanguinity, but is unlikely to show signs of phlegm, that being polar
opposite in the diagram. And so with the other temperaments.

Personal temperament may also be shaded by national temperament, or by the quality which belongs to a particular stage of life –
childhood being naturally sanguine, youth full of choleric will,
middle-age tinged with melancholy, and old-age having a phlegmatic
acceptance of life.

There is a danger, of course, in being too categorical in this matter, yet to recognize the temperament of a person is also to open the possibility of moving beyond the frictions that we might experience there towards a deeper encounter.

To return now to the writing – I am suggesting that there is some correspondence between these four temperaments and the four kinds of sentence that we have been considering.

Exercise 2

You can make the correspondence for yourself, and then see if there is any agreement between you. There is no ultimate answer; it can be seen from various viewpoints. I would perhaps see it like this:

Command	-	Choleric
Exclamation	-	Sanguine
Question	-	Melancholic
Statement	-	Phlegmatic

The last two, though, are somewhat problematic, as will be seen later.

This is no pedantic theory, however. The reality of the connection may well have been experienced in your attempt at *exercise 1*. A person with a sanguine temperament, for instance, will have great difficulty with the constraints of the statement, or a melancholic might find it hard to fill the command. You could examine the results of the exercise from this point of view – i.e. are your commands tinged with melancholy and doubt? – and come to some self-knowledge in the process. [This relation between style and temperament is taken up more fully on *p. 165*].

Earth, Water, Air and Fire

We have been exploring four different acts of language. As acts they can be enacted, prior to hanging any information on them.

Exercise 3

Draw the gestures of Statement, Question, Exclamation, Command [see *exercise 225*].

Exercise 4

Bring them into movement – e.g. in different ways of throwing a ball to each other [see *exercise 227*].

Exercise 5

Continue throwing, but name the qualities now according to the four elements of Earth, Water, Air, Fire.

This is a further connection I wish to make – that there is some correspondence between the sentence types and these four elements.

Exercise 6

Write down the correspondence as you experience it and then compare notes with others. Again there is no final answer. The order I mostly settle for is:

Fire	-	Command
Air	-	Exclamation
Water	-	Question
Earth	-	Statement

This does not quite tie in with the relationship made earlier with the temperaments, Melancholic being traditionally the earth temperament, and Phlegmatic the watery one. That is just as well! It saves us from the system.

Many exercises in this book are related to these elements – as subject-matter, style, qualities of movement, etc – and are gathered together on page 190. It is my central image, not imposed, I hope, but the recognition of a unity within the manifold.

I am indebted to Dr. Margaret Colquhoun for the further insight that these four elements, besides being states of matter to be passively observed, are also modes of looking at the world.[8] Beyond whatever basic attitude our temperament might give us we are free to choose the stance particularly suited to a situation, or to exercise all four elements (or sentence types) as progressive steps towards an understanding:

1. Standing before a thing – e.g. a thistle – I can assume an *earthy* attitude. I can measure it, *observe* its facts, draw it exactly, make *statements* about it without personal involvement.

2. I can observe it, not statically but as a thing in movement, in time – how one leaf form progresses to another up the stem; and by becoming *fluid* inwardly I can *imagine* the forms invisible between. I can ask *questions* about relationships.

3. I can stand before the plant and let its gesture and colour fall upon my open soul. I can observe (beyond what I impose as passing mood) the feelings that arise in me in response, and can sense what

quality in the universe is expressed here, what *air* it has about it. To grasp this means being willing to wait within the openness of a question until *inspiration* (followed by *exclamation*) comes. The picture of Adam on the front cover shows this moment of the process.

4. Now, having enlivened my thinking and perception through this progression, I can say, yes, this thing is indeed 'a thistle' – but here the naming is not the mere labelling of the earthy mode; it is an *intuitive* grasping of the whole, a confirmation of its unique existence [see *p. 23*]. This is the *fiery* mode, the mode of *command*.

The middle four sections of this book follow the same progression, taking language as its object [see also *p. 189*]. Ultimately, I would say, we are practising resurrection here, attempting to roll the stone from the tomb of our perception and of our speaking.

Image, sound, movement

Hidden within the fourfoldness that we have been concerned with is a threefoldness which relates to another aspect of the human being:

The section on Statement is mainly an exploration of the use of **imagery**.

The section on Exclamation explores the **sounding** of the language; word-music.

The section on Command has to do with **movement** and rhythm.

Image, Sound, Movement – these are the basic ingredients of poetry.

Further to this I have suggested –

Statement and image (word) come to expression in the **noun**:

    e.g. *This is a door.*

Exclamation and sound (syllable) are related to the **adjective**;

    e.g. *What a beautiful door!*

Command and movement (sentence) are connected to the **verb**:

    e.g. *Shut the door!*

Exercise 7

Write three pieces: one emphasizing Noun, one indulging Adjective, and one in which you give yourself over to Verb [see *exercise 272*]

Karl König in his book, *The First Three Years of the Child*,[9] points out that in the first year of a child's life it achieves freedom of movement, starting with the head, then the trunk, till finally the limbs are co-ordinated. In the second year freedom in speaking is achieved – first the nouns (which he relates to the head), then the adjectives (related to the heart), then finally the verbs (related to the limbs), and so the whole sentence is present. Perhaps this is a little simplified, for a child saying 'milk' is using what we call a noun to speak a whole sentence. Nonetheless, if he is right in relating noun, adjective and verb (the three main parts of speech) to our faculties of thinking, feeling and willing then, again, working with them we are exercising three ways of relating to the world. Grammar becomes 'Gramaire' – ensouled and human.

Exercise 8

Write a sentence which includes description, feeling and action:

> e.g. *The beautiful stallion raced across the plain and disappeared, far, far in the distance.*

Then read it in various ways:

Leaving out the adjectives –

> e.g. *The stallion raced across the plain and disappeared in the distance.*

Leaving out the verbs –

> e.g. *The beautiful stallion across the plain, far, far in the distance.*

Leaving out the nouns –

> e.g. *The beautiful raced across and disappeared, far, far.*

Exercise 9

Describe the place where you are

a) Without any limitations on the language.
b) Using no adjectives.
c) Using no verbs:

e.g. *Glass. Class. Clouds. Loud voice outside the door. Floor. Four girls. One boy with curls. One book of Miracles. Pink and yellow, grey and brown. A world of nouns. A frown. A footstep. Table askew. Sky, blue and thin. The blue veins under my skin. Her necklace neckless.*

d) Using no nouns. (This is almost impossible because adjectives and verbs keep consolidating into nouns. Let them):

e.g. *See through into the greening. Windy moving. We are here. All four. We lean towards the white rectangular that that is before us. Write write black wordingly. We are worldly here. The drink-from-see-through stands alone empty. Two girlings pink and blue. Two boyish ones white and wine. I hear who's footstepping there – the strangely ones back and forth beyond the knock knock. Who's that tonguing far away? There's no notioning. Who cares? We within what walls us are happy word-making.*

e) You can also try leaving out the nouns, adjectives and verbs altogether and work with what is in between. Pronouns are allowed, no doubt.

Just as we can come to know someone through the quality of their absence, so, relating to the world through these limitations, we can experience the qualities of noun, adjective and verb more clearly.

The Logos

It is most important that the structure of this book, as it has been described here, should be taken as a map for a journey, rather than any rigid system to be adhered to.

At my most inspired moments, actually, I have felt it to be no dry scheme at all, but an apprehension of the creative and ordering power of the Logos which exists prior to any concept of division between 'inner' and 'outer' and which works its numbers into the tiniest particulars of our existence.

Many people today have developed a deep concern for the Earth, and feel Nature's wounds as their own, but how many realize that language too is involved in this eco-logy (this 'house-logos')? Since Linguistics became an 'objective' science it is no longer respectable to refer to language as a living organism which can flourish or die according to how we nurture it, yet in working with these four sentence types it has seemed to me that we are touching upon what I can only call the life-structure of the language:

Statement: Question: Exclamation: Command

– these are the four springs that run out of Eden, carrying truth, interest, beauty, goodness (life-enhancing virtues) into our dealings with each other and with the world. If, however, through a broken or a trivial word, we pollute those sources then there is no doubt that the external rivers too will soon be full of it. At this point the contrast between 'word-poetry' and 'life-poetry' becomes irrelevant – both language and human life can be renewed here.

Two

The Statement

STATEMENT is the act of naming, describing, defining, of giving information about the state of things, its ideal being to name truly and with clarity – to be correct and wise.

Exercise 10
Place an object on the table. Ask everyone in the group to make a silent naming (or stating) gesture towards it. Observe what kind of a gesture it is. Here naming as an act becomes visible in its many aspects of indicating, measuring, stating, giving, limiting, etc.

Exercise 11
Name the object aloud in as many languages as you know. Look at the object through the name. A name as a label can certainly stand between us and our perception of an object, and yet to see oak, ash, elm, where others see only trees is surely a help to us. Which of the names that you came up with touches the closest?

Exercise 12
Make statements about the object – true ones, false ones, wise ones, foolish ones.

A statement is a type of sentence, of course (it is that aspect of sentence which the dictionary defines as a 'complete meaning'), but its primary aspect of bringing meanings and images to mind is already present in the single word, particularly in the nouns. Statements have the tendency to point towards the noun. Their favourite verb is 'to be'.

This section of the book, then, is basically concerned with the use of image and imagination – those aspects of language of which we are most conscious. More asleep in us are the sounds and movements of the language (we will deal with them in detail later), but if we start with the meanings we will find ourselves making music anyway.

Exercise 13
In the present moment and place (where, hopefully, there is a window), and using your senses of seeing, hearing, smelling, touching, tasting, name what is around you – random impressions. Things. The relationship between things. What things and people are doing. Don't pass too easily over the things you cannot name. Try to see what nobody else sees. As far as possible stay with impression rather than expression – i.e. don't, at this stage, interpret what you experience: e.g.

> *Adrian strokes his chin. A sigh from the girl in green. A cup without a handle. Red hat with a bobble. Scrape of a chair across wooden floor. One light off – light-holder lightless.*

Vivienne is left-handed. Duncan holds his nose as he writes.
Eyes looking around. Sound of coffee swallowed. Tinkle of
spoon and birdsong. The trees all leafless.

Such a naming of things can be practised in your mind as you go about
your daily business.

Read out now what you have written. Although everyone shared the
same place and moment and were set the same task, everyone (being
different) will surely have either selected different impressions or
described the same thing in their individual way.

Try to make conscious what these differences are: i.e. senses used;
words chosen for their sounds; individual rhythms; vague or detailed;
singular or plural; awareness of colour; interest in nature or in man-
made objects; verbs, adjectives or the lack of; use of metaphor and
personification; static or dynamic etc., and what might have caused
these differences: i.e. position in room; nationality; sex; mood;
temperament; previous reading; constitution etc. [see *p. 164*]

When you share such pieces it will be clear that total objectivity is
impossible, though some will succeed more than others. It is not a
matter of success or failure, but of recognizing differences and
revealing possibilities in use of language and imagery.

Outer things naturally embody inner qualities, and so in the reading
of these pieces mood will be conveyed, the beginnings of a poetry.
Between the impression and the writing something intervenes to lead it
towards expression in varying degrees. Seeking to name the outer we
begin to name inner things also.

[To make this relationship of outer to inner explicit this exercise can
be followed immediately by *exercise 77* where 'I am' is placed before the
things named].

It is important to realise that although words are about the world
(particularly in their aspect as statement) they are also powers.
Statement is the power that human beings have to name differences, to
distinguish between I and you, dark and light, cat and cabbage – not to
be lost in the primal mingle.

In the beginning God created the heaven and the earth. And the earth was
without form and void; and darkness was upon the face of the deep. And the
spirit of God moved upon the face of the waters. And God said, 'Let there be
light', and there was light. [1]

(*Genesis* Ch.1.)

Though we may lack the divine power to create light by naming it, we do nonetheless have the power, through naming, to create inner pictures in the minds of those who read or hear our words; to cloud or to enlighten. This is a major responsibility that we bear when using language, and it could be taken up as a conscious practice in the group throughout its work together.

Exercise 14

The previous exercise in naming can be led further into complete sentences and paragraphs. Still keep within the act of statement with its clarity of description – e.g.

> *The watch with the broken strap is on the table. The fat orange candle is on the table. The oblong table is in the oblong room. Paul likes the oblong room with the coloured wall. So does Pamela. Pamela is a girl. Silas is a boy. So is Nick. Silas has a blue and white pen. He writes words with it. These people used not to be in the oblong room but now they are. Nick has curly hair and a checked shirt. Silas has a stripy waistcoat. Paul wishes he had a stripy waistcoat. Everyone has elbows, even Pamela. There are eight elbows in this oblong room. 'Elbow' and 'oblong' are somehow similar. Oblong was the favourite word of my friend Paul Evans. Paul Evans is not here, though. He is elsewhere. I am here. So are we. Nick and Silas and Pamela and Paul. We all have names and we are here. We all have different names but are in one place. This is a good place. We are good people.*

Or it can be done from a painting [see *exercise 1*]. Notice how it veers towards exclamation as soon as feeling becomes involved.

In that first verse from the book of *Genesis* naming is seen to be a creative deed; the name of the thing and the thing named are one. By naming light God calls light into being. Later in the story we find that Adam (made in the image of God) has a similar power:

> *And out of the ground God formed every beast of the field and every fowl of the air; and brought them unto Adam to see what he would call them; and whatsoever Adam called every living creature that was the name thereof.*[2]

(*Genesis*, Ch. 2)

Each creature stands before him as a riddle and he must name it.

A Hebrew legend enlarges upon this by relating that when Adam was created some of the Angels had great difficulty understanding the

reason for his existence. Jahve, seeing this, brought the plants and
animals before them and asked if they could name them. The Angels
were quite unable to do so. Adam, however, could not only name the
plants and animals, but could speak his own name too, and even the
name of God. When the Angels heard this they began to understand
why human beings had been created.

The great modern German poet, Rainer Maria Rilke, had the same
intuition that naming is the essential human act:

> *Are we, perhaps, here just for saying: House,*
> *Bridge, Fountain, Gate, Jug, Fruit Tree, Window –*
> *possibly: Pillar, Tower? ... but for saying, remember,*
> *Oh, for such saying as never the things themselves*
> *hoped so intensely to be.*

To name them – not just for our own sake, but because

> *The Springs have need of you. Many a star*
> *was waiting for you to perceive it. Many a wave*
> *would rise in the past to meet you; or else perhaps*
> *as you went by an open window, a violin*
> *would be utterly giving itself. All this was commission.* [3]
>   (from the *Duino Elegies*, trans. Leishman and Spender)

Things commission us to name them. Through naming we have the
power to confirm people and things in their existence (something very
different from the male dominance over nature that Adam's deed is
often taken to represent).

Exercise 15
The poet Shelley said that 'poets are God's spies'. [4] Go out into the
world, then, and spy on it. Not with a cold eye, though, but with
wonder. Let whoever walks past walk into your writing. Transcribe
the event. Inner events can be included now, but keep it anchored to
what comes through the senses. [e.g. *p. 29*]

Epiphanies

In a recent spy case simple things such as a blue drawing pin at the top
of the stairs at Piccadilly Underground Station were said to be
messages left by secret agents. Just so, things which we dismiss as
unworthy of notice might in fact be messages left for us by the Muse.

Children have that quality of perception whereby they are able to
spy into the heart of things: e.g.

As I was swinging on my swing
On Advent morning the birds did sing.
I saw the cat a-staring in my eyes.
I saw my mother making pumpkin pies.

'Epiphanies', James Joyce called such moments.

Jean Cocteau: *Do you know the surprise of finding yourself suddenly facing your own name as if it belonged to someone else, seeing its form and the sound of its syllables without the blind and deaf habit which a long intimacy provides? The same phenomenon can take place for an object or an animal. In a flash we* **see** *a dog, a cab, a house for the first time. What is special, mad, ridiculous, beautiful in them is overwhelming. But immediately afterwards, habit rubs out this powerful image with its eraser. We pat the dog, hail the cab, inhabit the house. We don't see them any more.*
This is the role of poetry. It unveils, in the full meaning of the term. It strips bare, under a light which shatters our indifference, the surprising things around us which our senses register automatically.[5]

(from *Le Secret Professional*, trans. Wallace Fowlie)

This experience of seeing into the life of things, into the Name, is strong in Chinese and Japanese culture:
     The Japanese poet Basho says:

Go to the Pine if you want to learn about the Pine, or to the Bamboo if you want to learn about the Bamboo. And in doing so, you must leave your subjective preoccupation with yourself. Otherwise you impose yourself on the object and do not learn. Your poetry issues of its own accord when you and the object have become one – when you have plunged deep enough into the object to see something like a hidden glimmering there. However well phrased your poetry may be, if your feeling is not natural – if the object and yourself are separate – then your poetry is not true poetry but merely subjective counterfeit.[6]

The expression of such 'epiphanies' is well served by the Japanese Haiku form [see *exercise 245*]. Here is a description by one of Basho's disciples of how the most famous Haiku of all (rather loosely translated here) came to be written.

Breaking the silence
Of an ancient pond,
A frog jumped into water –
A deep resonance.

This poem was written by our master on a spring day. He was sitting in his riverside house in Edo, bending his ears to the soft cooing of a pigeon in the quiet rain. There was a mild wind in the air, and one or two petals of cherry blossom were falling gently to the ground. It was the kind of day you often have in late March – so perfect that you want it to last for ever. Now and then in the garden was heard the sound of frogs jumping into the water. Our master was deeply immersed in meditation, but finally he came out with the second half of the poem:

> *A frog jumped into water –*
> *A deep resonance.*

One of the disciples sitting with him immediately suggested for the first half of the poem,

> *Amidst the flowers*
> *Of the yellow rose.*

Our master thought for a while, but finally he decided on

> *Breaking the silence*
> *Of an ancient pond.*

The disciple's suggestion is admittedly picturesque and beautiful but our master's choice, being simpler, contains more truth in it. It is only he who has dug deep into the mystery of the universe that can choose a phrase like this.[7]

The difference between the disciple's version and Basho's points to the difference between description and evocation. It is a fine example of a 'true image' as defined by Ezra Pound, in that it 'presents an intellectual and emotional complex in an instant of time.'[8]

Our most immediate source of image is what comes to our eyes in the present moment. But there are other sources, each with their particular quality, waiting to be named and stated. An important one is

Memory

Exercise 16
Describe (orally) the view out of your bedroom window when you were nine years old, so vividly that others can also visualize it. On the next day someone else can describe the memory of that memory.

Exercise 17
Remember a place known to the whole group; describe a particular doorhandle, door, even the sound it makes.

Exercise 18
Describe, from memory, a person known to you.

Exercise 19
Remember what people in the group were wearing the last time you met, and where they were sitting.

Exercise 20
A helpful exercise to train this faculty is to go back over your day before going to sleep, visualizing it, but without emotional involvement. It can help you to observe more carefully on the following day.

Exercise 21
At the beginning of each group session it can be helpful to recall the content of what was written the time before. If you cannot remember, that is also significant.

Exercise 22
Write an 'I remember' piece – either random impressions, or one leading to another. They do not have to be deep confessions about your life. The aim here is to give vivid details, including names of people. There is no need to interpret or philosophize about the memories: e.g.

I remember the morning we found our white rabbit frozen to death in her hutch. I remember the old gardener showing me some artichokes and his withered knuckles looked exactly like them. I remember catching tadpoles. One dropped on the path and wriggled for a while all covered with dust. I remember trying to revive a dead fish, watching it float round in a bucket of water. I remember the hollow ringing my feet made on the iron fire-escape. I remember eating a fishcake. I remember my grandmother forcing me to drink a mixture of milk and Lucosade because it was good for me. I remember the school corridor. Jumping up I could touch the ceiling, and I left a dirty patch there with my hand. I remember the glass paper-weight on my grandfather's desk, and how the knights in his chess set had removable heads and needed gluing. I remember the giant squirrels who lived in the passage halfway up the stairs, but I was too quick for them. I remember Mrs. Beetroot who talked to herself. I remember the smell of plasticine trodden into the coconut matting. I remember the Emperor. Every day in the playground I was his slave. I remember chasing Harriet. I remember being one of the three kings. I remember the sound my bedroom door made and the metal coathangers clanging behind it. I remember the smell of my first history book and the picture of Charles I walking to his execution. I remember the deep pit we dug in the garden and how the bottom filled up with water but we sat in it anyway pretending to be soldiers. I remember the drinking fountain near the sandpits. I remember the pink cardigan of the woman who tried to teach me how to ice-skate. I remember our car passing a gap in the hedge through which I saw a man jumping off a tractor but he never reached the ground. And I remember a swarm of bees on the peartree. [9]

A remembered image often has a special light around it, more charged with feeling than the impressions that come to us 'in the light of common day'.

Another approach is that of Sei Shónagon, a 10th century Japanese Lady of the court who, in her *Pillow Book*, catalogued things she remembered under such titles as

> *Things that give a hot feeling.*
> *Things that fall from the sky.*
> *Things that have lost their power.*
> *Things that are distant though near.*

e.g. *Squalid things:*

The back of a piece of embroidery. The inside of a cat's ear. A swarm of mice who have no fur when they come wriggling out of their nest ... [10]

Exercise 23
Write such a title on a piece of paper and pass it round for each person to write one or two examples: e.g.

> *Things that Startle:*
>
> *Bright red hats.*
> *Mice in the night.*
> *Sudden sunshine in a grey English sky.*
> *The sudden unexpected decision.*
> *Paris underground.*
> *High voices on old heads.*
> *Footsteps and shooting stars.*
> *A worm in an apple.*
> *New ideas and naked women.*
> *The child that jumps from behind the door.*
> *The sudden thought that this is the wrong train.*
> *The last leaf falling from the tree on a clear winter's day.*

A scream in the dead of night.
A loud 'hello' from behind while vacuuming.
Too much salt in the soup.
Someone smiling at me in the London underground.
A candle on the window-sill setting the curtain on fire.
Electric light at dawn.

Remembered things are seen here through a particular mood or feeling.

Exercise 24
Centre upon one small area of your memory and explore it in writing. You could try it in written conversation with a partner, allowing yourself to be drawn out concerning the details.

Biography, obviously, is a major source of writing. In a close working group you could spend some time sharing your biographies.

William Wordsworth in his preface to the *Lyrical Ballads* says:

I have said that Poetry is the spontaneous overflow of powerful feelings; it takes its origin from emotion recollected in tranquillity: the emotion is contemplated till by a species of reaction the tranquillity gradually disappears, and an emotion similar to that which was before the subject of contemplation, is gradually produced, and does itself actually exist in the mind. In this mood successful composition generally begins...[11]

Exercise 25
Take a walk together as a group (preferably in a park or garden) knowing that upon return all that happens – what is seen, what is said – is to be transcribed from memory. It could be regarded as a ritual walk, a composing in action, a true bio-graphy (i.e. 'life-writing'), inscribed into the book of life. It could even be prepared beforehand, with hidden things and messages to be found. Set tasks for each other, language thresholds to be crossed – like telling a lie or a truth before crossing a stile, confessing a crime or an embarrassing moment, saying a word that you are afraid of.

Exercise 26
Transcribe the event from memory: e.g.

I walked down
to see what the gardeners do in winter.
No one was there.
Looking back I saw that the lights

had come on in the big house.

I took out my pencil and paper
and wrote: 'An old toolshed.
   The scarecrow's clothes
   are piled here for the winter.'

Then a gun went off. It startled me
in that still place.

Then Esther came along and I was shy
to be a poet in a shed and said
Esther do you mind it?

'The girl with the wheelbarrow,
gave me permission
to write
these words about her.'

The barrow sounded emptier as she trundled off.

It was so silent there. 'You too
   could be as full
   as a blue rainbarrel.'

Through the trees I could see a girl and a door.
It was the house calling me home.

No, no. 'Here on this chopping block
   let me rest
   my life a while.'[12]

This example is, in fact, a mixture of the exercise here suggested and the 'God's spies' exercise [*exercise 15*]. It is in the manner of the Japanese poet Basho who, in his *Narrow Road to the Deep North*, includes haiku written on the journey, with linking narrative passages that were written later from memory.

Exercise 27
Take a blindfold walk, being led by a partner. Upon return compose together out of your shared impressions.

Exercise 28
At the end of your working together as a group write an 'I remember' piece, based upon your time together, including what you thought but didn't say, remembering what people said and did. This can be done individually or with a partner, or even orally, writing down whatever is spoken.

Exercise 29
This can also be done in the form of a letter. Write 'Dear Sally,' (or whatever your name is) on a piece of paper and then pass it round for everyone to add a comment or a memory about your part in the group.

Such a gathering of threads can be very important.

Paintings and photographs

These are another source of images.

Exercise 30
Work, orally, from a painting, with such leading phrases as 'I see ...' or 'I think that ....' – an exercise in the observation of things and of the relationships between them.

A painting is a window of sorts, the artist heightening the significance of what we see there through selection and composition. Because of this, working from paintings can be a helpful way into the imaginative life. Good sources are Vermeer, Breughel, The Pre-Raphaelites – pictures with plenty of details.

Other exercises relating to paintings are suggested elsewhere.

Exercise 31
In the present context, write a descriptive piece from a painting, naming all the details and the relationships between them. e.g. from a painting by Jan Vermeer:

> *The man with the black rimmed hat has given the girl a drink of water out of a white jug.*
>
> *She is drinking it.*
>
> *Her nose is visible through the glass.*
>
> *The man looks anxiously to see whether she is enjoying his water.*
>
> *She is.*
>
> *She doesn't put it down to breathe.*
>
> *Her lute is on the chair resting on a blue cushion.*
>
> *The fact that he cares so much about her enjoyment of this water shows that he loves her.*
>
> *He is her music teacher – and he loves her.*

She is visiting his house.
He is giving his lesson in the dining-room.
The light on his face is not from the window
but because he is wondering whether to smile.
When the girl finishes her drink he is going
to offer her another.
And when she has finished that he will ask
to marry her, and she will say 'you ... but you
are my music teacher' and he will say 'yes but
I'd break my lute for you for you I'd cut off
all the strings'.
And she in her confusion pours another glass
of water. [13]

Exercise 32 (set by Leonardo da Vinci):

You should look at certain walls stained with damp, or at stones of uneven colour. If you have to invent some setting you will be able to see in these likenesses of divine landscapes, adorned with mountains, ruins, rocks, woods, great plains, hills and valleys in great variety; and then again you will see there battles and strange figures in violent actions; expressions of faces and clothes and an infinity of things which you will be able to reduce to their complete and proper forms. In such walls the same thing happens as in the sound of bells, in whose strokes you may find every word which you can imagine. [14]

e.g.   *Leonardo would have loved this garden wall*
where the faces of nothing at all
move among ivies.
When Leonardo and I look through the same eyes
the shadows of ivy moving grow wilder
than any form ever walled in a garden.
My shadow splashed on the wall is all
mossed and ivied. I have seen gardens there
to rival the bright leaves of Leonardo's notebook.
Sunlight on this garden wall seems far
from any wars, Leonardo; yet even here
there are captains mustering the ivy shadows.
To move through the garden with Leonardo's eyes
is to find all the smiles you wish for
in the Louvre of ivy.

a young

bull breaks

the gates down

and is tame suddenly
having nowhere to go.
The prairie tastes no
sweeter than the grass
inside his paddock. Human he would
cry now. The cloud reflected in his
eye would have to dissolve entirely
to escape horizons.

Cattle skulls. And a broken fence. A
pistol? The wood bleeds. Shadows break
loose from their objects. And beyond
this? Nothing. Having chanced here.
An abandonned place. A few scraps
cling to the bones. Enough to sustain
me one day. It's how I travel.

Phantasy

Exercise 33
Build up (orally) in the group an imagined scene full of vivid details.

Exercise 34
Through the power of phantasy you are able to know all that is
happening in the world at this moment. Write down, at random, some
of the things that you see and hear. It is important to see them inwardly
before you write: e.g.

*I see the reflection of a taxi moving across a shop window in Derby. I see a
dirty piece of string dangling from a boy's coat pocket. I see the darkness
inside his pocket. I see an eye on the other side of a keyhole. The eye sees me
and moves away, revealing a brightly lit room with a table laid for a feast
but no one is eating it. I see a block of flats. I see into each of its rooms. I see a
lonely man chewing a raisin. I see a woman leaning her elbows on the
windowsill watching the trains shunting about below and the moon rising*

behind the gasworks. I see a young girl hanging green socks on a clothesline. I see a wolf's skull lying on a shelf. I see a chaffinch carrying pieces of newspaper to make its nest. I see the torn photograph of a Hungarian ballet-dancer. I see myself feeling for something inside a huge wellington boot. I see what it is – a pale green stone held there in my hand.

Now, in the group, each choose one of those things seen and read them round. Notice which ones particularly light up in clarity and which are too general or too cluttered with adjectives. Test them, perhaps, by leaving out the adjectives.

Exercise 35

With a partner, enter a shared imagination of a place where things are happening (but hold it back from story.) Don't invent the place; discover it together in the writing. The immediacy of such discovery is helped if you write in the present tense. Then try it by yourself. e.g.

This is the place where someone lost a glove. A green glove. It lies here on the green grass. A left glove. A child's left glove. It lies here wet in the green grass with the thumb bent under. Both grass and glove are wet. The beads of water hang upon the strands of wool, and a small spider stands upon the pointing finger. A small dark spider without a face. It is not moving. The glove is not moving, but the short grass moves a little as the wind moves over it. The grass is green. The wind is colourless. The glove has the look of something lost. Its green is darker than the place it is lost in. If the other glove were here it would seem less lost. The other is not here. It is elsewhere and leaves its absence here beside the other. This is true, and the spider moves to another finger. The two greens darken as a cloud shadow passes. No other thing is told about this place.

The scene can be bigger than that. The aim of the exercise is to achieve clarity of image rather than to create atmospheric effects. In extreme cases emotive adjectives could be forbidden.

John Keats, at the end of his Ode, 'To the Nightingale', flies off on the 'viewless wings of Poesy', so far, that in his imagination he comes right to the edge of eyesight where a 'magic casement' (or window) opens 'on the foam of perilous seas in faerylands forlorn.'

Exercise 36

If you are prepared to brave that peril you could take the Celtic *Voyage of Maelduin* as a model for writing, adding to the list of islands that he visited some islands of your own. e.g.

- an island where the sea hurls salmon through a stone valve into a house.
- an island with a Wondrous Beast, which can turn its body round inside its skin and revolve its skin round its body.
- an island with an arch of water, like a rainbow full of salmon, rising on one side of it and falling on the other.[15]

Or it could be a magical 'room where ....'

This brings us to the beginnings of story-making. Out of statement the Epic mode arises.

Wondrous sight

Many people do indeed experience this realm of phantasy as 'perilous.' Thresholds always are. Why else would Angels say, 'fear not', whenever they make an appearance? And yet, if we are to come to certain levels of truth we have to take risks with the literal, and be silly. Actually, the word 'silly' derives from the German 'seelig', meaning 'blessed' or 'soulful'. That is as much as to say that you will not come to the sacred unless you are prepared to make a fool of yourself.

Exercise 37
If you need an excuse to be silly, imitate the form of this nursery rhyme:

> *I saw a peacock with a fiery tail*
> *I saw a blazing comet drop down hail*
> *I saw a cloud with ivy curled around*
> *I saw a sturdy oak creep on the ground*
> *I saw an ant swallow up a whale*
> *I saw a raging sea brim full of ale*
> *I saw a Venice glass sixteen foot deep*
> *I saw a well full of men's tears that weep*
> *I saw their eyes all in a flame of fire*
> *I saw a house high as the moon and higher*
> *I saw the sun at twelve o'clock at night*
> *I saw the man who saw this wondrous sight.*

Another, similar, example ends with the lines:

> *I saw a man who saw these too*
> *And said though strange they all were true.*

Yes, they are all true, because it is possible to read them from the middle of one line to the middle of the next, whereby they all become quite sensible. There is, however, a deeper truth sometimes in that which at first seems foolish. The man who sees the sun at midnight, for instance, is one who attains to mystic vision, indeed arriving at 'wondrous sight' beyond the literal. When reading out examples take note of those lines which are particularly striking, and consider why.

Exercise 38
Try the same exercise, but without the repetition at the beginning of each line: e.g.

> *The sea formed beautiful shapes / in your hair and face*
> *I'd love to touch and to smell / the empty space*
> *The world and I are one / in a cup of tea*
> *There is milk and sugar/ hidden in blood I see*
> *The first colour that men used to write....*
>   (Klass Hoffman)

Lying

Sometimes it is not enough to be exhorted to 'use your imagination'; we need to find ways of giving ourselves permission to do so – permission to be silly, permission to break down the inhibition against 'untruth' which can so often be a repression of the healthy life of phantasy:

Exercise 39
Write a truth: e.g.

God could fit inside a matchbox.

Exercise 40
Write a lie: e.g.

Blindmen can see further than anyone else.

Exercise 41
Write two truths and a lie about yourself. Ask others to guess which one the lie is.

Exercise 42
Write a whole page of lies: e.g.

I can hear the fleas singing 'God save the Queen', behind the ears of the cows in the field.

I can hear the second-hands on their wristwatches ticking.

My nose is so sensitive I can tell what kind of deodorant the mosquitoes in Panama are using.

[For an extension of this see *exercise 121* and *exercise 289*].

Paradox

The sentence – 'blindmen can see further than anyone else,' is not necessarily a lie, of course. It is a paradox which, on some level, contains a truth; in fact the Chinese sage Lao Tze says, 'paradox is the highest form of truth.' He gives an example:

Tao is a great square with no angles … a great sound that cannot be heard, a great image without form.[16]

Children also enjoy paradox and contradiction: e.g.

> *One fine day in the middle of the night*
> *Two dead men got up to fight.*
> *Back to back they faced each other,*
> *Drew their swords and shot each other.*

Exercise 43
Write some playful verses in a similar vein.

Exercise 44
Write some wise ones: e.g.

A long love must often amaze the heart by being brief.

[see also *exercise 134* and *exercise 295*].

Dreaming

Dreaming is a further source of image. We may doubt the value of the silly make-believe that we have been indulging in, yet in our dreams (whether we like it or not) we are all creators of 'ridiculous' images and stories. And, after all, modern psychologists would say that they are not so ridiculous really:

Exercise 45
'Dreams' – let's take that word and see what is hidden inside it: e.g.

> *Dreams Reveal Exactly All My Sorrows.*
> *Dreams rise even after meals sometimes.*
> *Dreams radiantly expand above my soul.*
> *Dreams richly enter a maiden's sleep.*
> *Dreams resolve ethical anxieties most specifically.*
> *Dreams resound ever answering my silence.*

Introducing the theme through such an exercise you can gather from the group (without much ado) many aspects of dreaming. Some dreams, it seems, arise out of bodily or psychological disturbance, whereas others come to us as revelations out of nowhere. Whatever direction they come from the dreamer in each of us is a consummate maker of symbols.

The question is – where might that symbol-maker be hiding while we are awake, and might it be possible (as Robert Duncan puts it) 'to open Night's Eye that sleeps in what we know by day'?[17]

Exercise 46
Make up a dream (maybe with a partner), finding the grammars that belong to it. Try to be inside the dream, present tense, not talking about it: e.g. (but in past tense)

A group of old men were sitting around a table, discussing. A black raven flew through the window and began to tell about Janita. Janita Wayne was waiting for the train but just as it arrived the horse was hungry and wouldn't move forward. We began to be afraid in case we would never leave. There were noises on the distant horizon invading the tranquillity of the sea-shore. We could see the black sails and the tide began to come in. The sand became soft and our feet sank in, like fingers kneading dough. The water came over our heads and the dough grew sticky. It was put in a warm place to rise while the children returned to their games. [see also *exercise 290*]

(Lynnice Yates)

Many great works of literature are made-up dreams – *Pilgrim's Progress*; *The Vision of Piers Plowman*; *Mrs. Tiggywinkle*. Sigmund Freud asked his patients to record their dreams for him, but when he discovered that some were fobbing him off with made-up dreams he soon realized that he could analyse those just as fruitfully. He had difficulty, however, in comprehending the work of the Surrealist poets who recognized in his dream theories new possibilities for the image. [see *p 48*].

Exercise 47
Any would-be poet would do well to write down dreams, and to pay attention to those moments between sleep and waking.

Sometimes not just images, but words, complete poems even, can be received out of sleep – as was Caedmon's Hymn to the Creator [*p 183*]. The most famous example in English poetry is *Kubla Khan*, by Samuel Taylor Coleridge. Concerning its composition, he wrote:

The author continued for about three hours in a profound sleep, at least of the external senses, during which time he has the most vivid confidence that he could not have composed less than two or three hundred lines, if that indeed can be called composition in which all the images rose up before him as things, with a parallel production of the correspondent expressions.[18]

When he came to publish his great poem, however, he presented it 'rather as a psychological curiosity, than on the ground of any supposed poetic merit' – an apology hardly to be reconciled with the supreme confidence and power of the inspired poet who figures in the last few lines of the poem –

> ..... *Beware, beware,*
> *His flashing eyes, his floating hair!*
> *Weave a circle round him thrice*
> *And close his eyes with holy dread,*
> *For he on honeydew hath fed,*
> *And drank the milk of paradise.*

The whole poem should be sought out. It moves beyond dream into being a myth of the creative process.

Naming (1)

So far we have been exercising clarity of naming and statement with regard to present perceptions of the outer world, memory, paintings, phantasy, dream, and looking towards fairy tale and myth (to be taken up in the final section).

So, what is naming? Basically, it is a twofold act – a pushing away of the world, and an establishing of relationship. This polarity is even declared to us in the very name of 'naming' –the 'N' sound expressing, 'no, it is not me, but a stone, a bus, an elephant,' or whatever, while the 'M' sound has more the quality of sympathy towards the world, and a recognition of its qualities.

These two aspects are actually embodied in the substance of the English language. Consider the following list of synonyms:

volition	-	*will*
cognition	-	*knowing*
osculation	-	*kissing*
amicable	-	*friendly*

Probably you would agree that the words in the left hand column (which come from Latin) are somewhat abstract and remote, whereas the words on the right (from Anglo Saxon) are much more down to earth and engaging – so earthy, in fact, that some Saxon words are considered 'obscene', and are not allowed in dictionaries.

Exercise 48
Find some other examples of synonyms, possibly contradicting what has just been said.

George Orwell, in his essay 'Politics and the English Language', was rather fierce about this difference. He quotes the following passage (which uses mainly Anglo-Saxon words):

I returned, and saw under the sun, that the race is not to the swift, nor the battle to the strong, neither yet bread to the wise, nor yet riches to men of understanding, nor yet favour to men of skill; but time and chance happeneth to them all.[19]

(*Ecclesiastes* Ch.9)

And compares it to:

Objective consideration of contemporary phenomena compels the conclusion that success or failure in competitive activities exhibits no tendency to be commensurate with innate capacity, but that a considerable element of the unpredictable must invariably be taken into account.[20]

Both passages convey the same message, but the second, couched as it is in Latinate words for the sake of 'objectivity', results in an unnecessary obscurity. It was Orwell's point that in the mouths of politicians and 'experts', such language is dangerous, so often being used as a means of hiding (or hiding from) the truth [see also *p. 127*].

Definition and characterization (1)

Sometimes a name is not enough to say what something is, so we
extend into longer definitions and characterizations. It is the same
polarity – a setting apart (definition), an establishing of relationship
(characterization), and any degree of either.

Exercise 49
Take a name and open it a little, finding what is folded inside: e.g.

rose

red rose

red rose on the bush

red rose with perfect petals on the green bush

rose with perfect petals and sharp thorns on the green bush

the sharp and perfect rose

the rose

Now try to speak the word 'Rose' in such a way that it contains within
it all the facts and mysteries that have been made explicit.

   The separating aspect of definition is caricatured by Charles
Dickens in his novel, *Hard Times*.[21] Mr. Gradgrind, inspector of
schools, is speaking to the teacher, Mr. McChokemchild:

*Now, what I want is facts. Teach these boys and girls nothing but facts.
Facts alone are wanted in life. Plant nothing else, and root out everything
else. You can only form the minds of reasoning animals upon facts; nothing
else will ever be of any service to them ....*

Later, in the classroom, he asks 'girl number 20' to give him the
definition of a horse. Finding her unable to do so he turns to a boy
called Bitzer, who supplies –

*Quadruped. Graminivorous. Forty teeth, namely twenty-four grinders,
four eye-teeth and twelve incisive. Sheds coat in the Spring; in marshy
countries sheds hoofs too. Hoofs hard, but requiring to be shod with iron.
Age known by marks in mouth.*

'Now girl number 20,' says Mr. Gradgrind, 'you know what a horse is.'
It is a true definition, for sure, true to the dead horse, but somehow
leaving the horse out – it denies all life and inwardness. This is the
Wooden Horse of the intellect which the Greeks infiltrated into the
ancient world.

Exercise 50
Now write a characterization of a horse, trying to find a language for

those aspects which Mr. Gradgrind, with his insistence upon 'facts', disregarded:

e.g. from the book of Job:

Hast thou given the horse strength? Hast thou clothed his neck with thunder? Canst thou make him afraid as the grasshopper? The glory of his nostrils is terrible. He paweth in the valley, and rejoiceth in his strength; he goeth on to meet the armed men. He mocketh at fear, and is not affrighted; neither turneth he back from the sword. The quiver rattleth against him, the glittering spear and the shield. He swalloweth the ground with fierceness and rage: neither believeth he that it is the sound of the trumpet. He saith among the trumpets, Ha! Ha! and he smelleth the battle afar off, the thunder of the captains and the shouting.[22]

Leonardo Da Vinci
'Rearing Horse'

The picture on the front cover, of Adam naming the animals, can set the right inner gesture for this exercise. His right hand alone might be Gradgrind's way; his left hand listens to another source entirely.

It is possible, of course, in redeeming Mr. Gradgrind to go to the other extreme and to smother the object with our emotions. This also brings us into untruth, i.e. sentimentality. Permit the thing to have its otherness, and yet use your imagination to express the quality that belongs to it. Imagination can indeed be a servant of the truth:

William Blake: *I see everything I paint in This World, but Everybody does not see alike. To the Eyes of a Miser a Guinea is more beautiful than the Sun, and a bag worn with the use of Money has more beautiful proportions than a Vine filled with Grapes. The tree which moves some to tears of joy is in the eyes of others only a Green thing that stands in the way. Some see Nature all Ridicule and Deformity, and by these I shall not regulate my proportions; and some scarce see Nature at all. But to the Eyes of the Man of Imagination, Nature is Imagination itself. As a man is, so he sees. As the eye is formed, such are its Powers. You certainly mistake, when you say that the Visions of Fancy are not to be found in This World. To me this world is all one continued Vision of Fancy or Imagination.*[23]

(from a letter to Dr. Trusler).

Such an Eye can be worked for:

Exercise 51
Speak, without premeditation, on a given subject – e.g. eyebrows, ginger, hedgehogs.

Exercise 52
Pass an object around the group, and each (orally) make an observation (not a personal association) about it. You can also place it in time, imagining back into its history.

Exercise 53
If the group has been together for some time you could give each other small gifts (suited to the recipient) and speak, or write, about what you have been given and what it means to you.

Exercise 54
Put some folded questions on the table – e.g. 'What is a door?' 'What is a moment?' and ask everyone to take one (it is best if 2 or 3 people receive the same question). Now define or characterize what you receive:

e.g. *What is a nose?*

1. *A thing with which we touch the air, carefully.*
2. *Something everyone has, big or small, nice or ugly. Sometimes we see further than it is long, and that's probably what we should do with it.*
3. *Where our eyes meet in the middle and become unclear about what they really see.*   (Ronald Beffers)

What is a poet?

A poet is sometimes a pot with an 'e' in its middle, and sometimes a pet with an 'o' in its middle; but most often it is a person with nothing in the middle trying to make something come out. (Jan Williams)

If the object is not named in the writing it can be read as a riddle. [see *p. 90*].

When the pieces are read out it will be clear that some people have been concerned about clarity of *communication,* whereas others have been more interested in fullness of *expression.*

Communication and expression – these are the two fundamental poles of language. They exist in dynamic relationship to each other.

'Girl number 20' (otherwise known as Sissy Jupe) could not satisfy Mr. Gradgrind because, being a child, she was unable to enter into adult abstractions. Here is an 8 year old girl's definition of a Grandmother:

A grandmother is a lady who has no children of her own, so she likes other people's boys and girls. Grandmas don't have anything to do except to be there. If they take us for walks they slow down past pretty leaves and caterpillars. They never say hurry up. Usually they are fat, but not too fat to tie our shoes. They wear glasses, and sometimes they can take their teeth out. They can answer questions like why dogs hate cats and why God isn't married. When they read to us they don't skip words or mind if its the same story over again. Everyone should try to have a grandma, especially if you don't have television, because Grandmas are the only grownups who always have time.

Exercise 55
Try, although it is impossible, to write such a childlike description.

Exercise 56
Or try to enter into how an 'uncivilized' person, without our modern abstract consciousness, might view the world:
    e.g. A mountain (from the Aztec):

High, pointed: it is pointed on top, pointed at the summit, towering; wide, cylindrical, round; a round mountain, low, low-ridged; rocky, with many rocks; craggy, with many crags; rough with rocks; of earth; with trees; grassy; with herbs; with shrubs; with water; dry; white; jagged; with a sloping plain, with gorges, with caves; precipitous; having gorges; canyon land, precipitous land with boulders. I climb the mountain. I scale the mountain. I live on the mountain. I am born on the mountain. No one becomes a mountain – no one turns himself into a mountain. The mountain crumbles. [24]

According to the dictionary a mountain is 'an elevation of the Earth's surface, large or high hill.' That may be useful if you want to go and dig gravel out of it; but this Aztec cannot separate himself from his mountain. He is defining its quality. He is defining himself. He contradicts himself. He repeats himself – grappling with the being of this mountain, trying to become the mountain, to become a mouth for it. Well, he says no one becomes a mountain, but by saying so he declares the struggle he is engaged in. As all poets must be engaged.

These definitions – by the child, by the primitive – are, like Job's Horse, wonderful *verb*-al evocations, overcoming Mr. Gradgrind's static facts.

Ernest Fenollosa (from *The Chinese Written Character as a Medium for Poetry*): *A true noun, an isolated thing, does not exist in nature. Things are only terminal points, or rather the meeting points, of actions, cross-sections cut through actions, snapshots. Neither can a pure verb, an abstract motion, be possible in Nature. The eye sees noun and verb as one – things in motion, motion in things. ... The cherry tree is all that it does. Its correlated verbs compose it.*[25]

Fenollosa's book was one of the main inspirations of the Imagist movement, which was started by Ezra Pound. A well known poem by a later Imagist, Wallace Stevens, is 'Thirteen Ways of Looking at a Blackbird,' in which a number of haiku type poems are strung together, each containing the word 'blackbird.'[26]

Exercise 57
Do the same, choosing some other subject:

e.g. *Three ways of looking at a toothbrush*

> *1.*
> *Reaching for you*
> *before rushing out the door.*
> *Your taste on my mouth,*
> *Oh toothbrush.*
>
> *2.*
> *In those days*
> *we shared a toothbrush*
>
> *3.*
> *The house seems bare*
> *since you came*
> *to collect your toothbrush.*
>   (Lindsay Dearlove)

Another way to approach the qualities of things is to explore *differences between*. Children delight in asking such questions as 'What's the difference between a Roman barber and an angry circus owner?' (One is a shaving Roman, the other a raving showman.) And if we, in contemplation, explore the difference between an oaktree and a willow tree, for example, or (more generally) between mineral, plant, animal and human, we can come to a wise childhood in which we apprehend things in relation to the whole.

Exercise 58
So, you can ask each other questions such as, 'What is the difference between' –

> a daffodil and a rose?
> a rose and a tiger?
> a ruby and a rose?
> a rose and a human being?

and answer them in writing.

Characterization through comparison

To make comparisons, to search out correspondences is a universal human urge. Children hold up their biscuit after every bite and ask what it looks like. Hamlet in his feigned madness asks Polonius – *'Do you see yonder cloud that's almost in the shape of a camel?'* *'By the mass, and 'tis like a camel indeed!'* *'Methinks it is like a weasel!'* *'It is backed like a weasel.'* Visual correspondences. But Hamlet is also implying some inner resemblance to Polonius, who is trying to weasel secrets out of him.[27]

Simile

Exercise 59
Give written questions to your neighbour, such as 'What is the moon like?' 'What is an oaktree like?' and then answer them:

   e.g. *An oaktree is like an ancient book.*

Exercise 60
Make your own version of this nursery rhyme:

There was a man of double deed
Sowed his garden full of seed.
When the seed began to grow,
'Twas like a garden full of snow;
When the snow began to melt,
'Twas like a ship without a belt;
When the ship began to sail,
'Twas like a bird without a tail;
When the bird began to fly
'Twas like an eagle in the sky;
When the sky began to roar,
'Twas like a lion at the door;
When the door began to crack,
'Twas like a stick across my back;
When my back began to smart,
'Twas like a penknife in my heart;
When my heart began to bleed,
'Twas death and death and death
indeed.

It is an exercise in the use of simile, and at the same time it approaches the magical act of the metaphor [see *p. 49*] – the ship that seems merely like a bird on one line actually becomes a bird in the next.

Synesthesia

Another form of simile is synesthesia, in which the experience of one of our physical senses is expressed in terms of another.

Exercise 61
Playfully, you can ask and answer questions such as 'What does the sound of churchbells taste like?' 'What does the smell of a rose sound like?'

Exercise 62
Seriously, you can write a free-flowing piece in which you explore the possibilities here, as does the French poet Baudelaire when in his poem, 'Correspondences', he speaks of

> *perfumes as cool as the flesh of children*
> *sweet as oboes, green as prairies.*[28]

or as Edith Sitwell does in

> *Jane, Jane,*
> *Tall as a crane,*
> *the morning light creaks down again.*[29]
> (from 'Aubade')

Someone who slipped over that threshold unprepared was Bottom in Shakespeare's *A Midsummer Night's Dream*:

I have had a most rare vision ... the eye of man hath not heard, the ear of man hath not seen, man's hand is not able to taste, his tongue to conceive or his heart to report, what my dream was.[30]

This is not so bizarre really. We use it all the time, in fact, when we speak of the tone of a colour, or of someone's fine artistic taste. [see also *exercise 204*]

Blazonning

Exercise 63
A basic correspondence you can work with is that between nature and the human body.

Men in their desire to express the beauty of a woman are constantly returning to this:
e.g. (from *The Song of Solomon*)

Behold thou art fair; thou hast dove's eyes within thy locks; thy hair is as a flock of goats that appear from Mount Gilead. Thy teeth are like a flock of sheep that are even shorn ...[31]

You have to be careful when making such comparisons, for a visual likeness may not always carry an emotional likeness. To our modern ears, for instance, the comparison of a woman's hair to a 'flock of goats' seems somewhat inappropriate. If we visualize it too strongly we are thrown right out of the thought of her beauty into some other scene.

Such comparisons easily become cliché, and Shakespeare, realizing this, turned the practice (which is known as 'blazonning) around by starting a sonnet:

> *My mistress' eyes are nothing like the sun,*
> *Coral is far more red than her lips red ...*[32]

and ended by saying that her beauty is more rare than any 'belied with false compare.'

Can the beauty of a man be expressed through the same comparison with nature? [see *p. 159* for a further example of blazonning].

André Breton, a leader of the Surrealist movement, has given new vigour to this genre in his poem, 'Free Union,' where he speaks of

>*My wife with her wood fire hair*
>*With her thoughts of heatsparks*
>*With her shape of an hour-glass*
>*My wife with her shape of an otter*
>>>*between the tiger's teeth ....*[33]

It is not clarity he is after here – 'Beauty will be convulsive or not at all,' he once wrote. There is a dynamic correspondence as well as a visual one.

Linking words and phrases with an 'of' was a favourite device of the Surrealist poets, something in between a simile and a metaphor, enabling them to achieve startling juxtapositions of image:

Exercise 64
In a playful way, try linking words or phrases with an 'of' between them. e.g.

>*agony of doors*
>*harp of rain*
>*grain of death*
>*jump of lavender*
>*salt of storms*

Exercise 65
Or, even more playfully, do it with a partner, folding the first word or phase: e.g.

>*an intention ....*
>*of tired buckets*

You can do better than that.

Exercise 66
This can be extended into a piece with a more definite focus – e.g. continuing in André Breton's way:

>*Your pockets of money and midnight*
>*Your pockets of silvery echo*
>*Your pockets of starlight and old string*
>
>*Your scarf of breezes*

Your scarf chequered yesterday and tomorrow
Your shirt stitched with an ancient silence

Your shoes of the ten commandments
Your shoes hammered with the crucifix
Your horizon shoes
Your shoes of beyond, of sky-leather

Your gloves of nothing
Your smile gloves
Your maybe hat
Your hat of birdsong and thunder

Your waistcoat of sleek water
Your buttons of predictable eclipse
Your leaf-shadow jacket
Your jacket of half-truths with a patched elbow
Your subterranean coat
Your coat of the earth-filled grave.

Metaphor

Exercise 67
Take one of the similes you made (a cliché will do)

e.g. *Your eyes are like stars.*

and move it towards metaphor, at first just by removing the word 'like'.

e.g. *Your eyes are stars.*

On a literal level, of course, the simile has more truth in it. But how much more exciting to be told that your eyes *are* stars. Here is that threshold again where, to find a language for more inward truths, we must risk our fixed adult concepts.

Exercise 68
A playful way of opening to metaphorical thinking is the following: each write one adjective and two nouns on separate pieces of paper. Now pass one noun to your right, the adjective to your left and, with the adjective and noun that you receive, define the noun that you kept in front of you. e.g.

> *castle = square echo*
> *beauty = blowing open*
> *butterfly = passionate air*
> *air = mute remembering*
> *passion = blue dignity*
> *passion = majestic thorn*
> *grief = transparent thorn*
> *essence = tiny clarity*

Exercise 69

Write, metaphorically, what the moon is:

e.g. *The moon is a tired ballet-dancer.*

After you have written a number like that you can begin to bury the metaphor deeper – into the verbs.

e.g. *The moon dances on the rooftops.*

Consider in the group which ones are true to the quality of the moon (for that is the aim), and which are just being poetic. Is the moon 'he' or 'she'? Is there truth in such a comparison?

  The moon is an image which has been greatly overworked in poetry – 'the moon is a cliché,' in fact. Nevertheless it is surely part of any poet's initiation to declare a relationship to her. In Greek mythology she has a threefold aspect – maiden, mother and whore – seemingly contradictory. Yet that is the moon's nature – to give back whatever light is shone upon her. She will accept almost anything you say about her, and for that reason is indeed a good anvil on which to forge your metaphors.

Exercise 70

Remove the definite and indefinite articles from your moon metaphors, e.g.

> *The moon is last chapter*
> *The moon is ship and shadow*
> *The moon is lovely slumberer*
> *The moon is elbow*
> *The moon is bone echo*
> *The moon is yellow howler*

In this way the metaphor goes even deeper. It becomes a new name. [see *exercise 129; exercise 130*].

Many of the exercises suggested in this book make use of a simple repetitive form. Once that has got you started, however, you can break free from it: e.g.

The Moon is a Mirror.

The poet, thinking to define her, finds only
himself, snared there in the loops of his pen.

The moon is a broken rocking-horse.
The moon is a pick-pocket. The moon is

whatever a man calls her because that man,
naming her, names truly himself.

The moon is a girl. The moon
is a widow tying her shoelace.

The moon
is imagination itself, and shows us
the nature of our own imaginings.

And some at full moon must be restrained lest
their own unacknowledged nature destroys them.

Does the moon think that all poets love her?

How could we when she turns
our photographs brown at the edges?

But we did love her
with her former complexion.

Every statement about the moon
returns as a question.
Has she lost her powder-puff?

The moon is a harlequin, sad,
painted with a borrowed light.

And though I contradict myself the moon
who's a constant shift to the opposite
resolves it. And though I said
she was a girl before
she's an old whore
winking in the bars.

She eludes definition.

The moon is the poet's anvil. The moon
is a continuous arrival. [34]

Exercise 71
Now choose your own subject as a basis for extended metaphor.

Personification

Working with the image of the moon you will soon find yourself referring to it as 'he' or 'she' – that is, you will start to personify the world of so-called inanimate objects.

William Wordsworth in his Preface to the *Lyrical Ballads* says: *In these poems I propose to myself to imitate and, as far as possible to adopt, the very language of men, and I do not find that such personification makes any regular or natural part of that language.*[35]

It is a strange conclusion to come to. Children are always saying, 'Goodbye, House,' or 'Hello, Mrs. Spider'. It would seem to be a natural need to personify, to measure nature by what is human. As soon as language begins to express feelings it moves towards personification, things being seen to act with intent – a leaf shakes 'timidly', a storm comes 'raging' over the hill. It can certainly become an unnatural literary device, yet it was once a living experience for people that nature was filled with being and intelligence. It was clear to them that under the husk of things lurked the gnomes, undines, sylphs and salamanders – the beings of the elements.

The conflict between child and adult, modern and primitive, heart and head, is one that the poet continually has to work with.

One of the permissions granted in this book is that you may talk to things:

Exercise 72
Write a few sentences, or a letter, addressing an object as though it were a person: e.g.

Dear Door,

Here I am, sitting in this room, and there you are, brown and wooden. I am quite happy here. Not always, though. Sometimes I wait for a knock to come. Or for a letter pushed under you. I look at you. Maybe you look at me too – but you never smile. You look in and you look out – both ways. Sometimes I put my ear to you, listening for the voices out there. Sometimes those voices stop and look at me through your keyhole. You, Door, are such a patient person – you have an honest look. If I were a door I'd be just a little afraid – to live in that nowhere place between out and in. I am at home here inside with my books, and

*outside the world is on its way. One day a great knock knock will come, and I'll
say no no, I have one more book to read, one letter to write. Be a strong door
then; don't laugh at me and my small comforts.*

> Yours,
> Alice Barnett.

Exercise 73

Write a reply to the letter, taking on the voice of the object. Or choose
an object, and speak for it. Don't impose your own voice – lend it, and
help that object become articulate: e.g.

*Window: I always see you, but you rarely seem to notice me. I'm just there.
You usually pass me by without admiring, and seem to look right through
me. You pass by, unaware of how I keep you warm and bring you light. It's
true, I sometimes distort the truth for you, colouring or clouding your vision,
but I do need some amusements.*

If read without its title it would be something of a riddle [see *p. 90*], yet
another form of characterization. And perhaps, after all, the writer is
saying something about herself through the object she has chosen.

Exercise 74

Another interesting approach is to take a smell, or two contrasting
smells (e.g. sage and rosemary), and characterize them as persons –
young or old, male or female, large or small, shy or strident etc.
Sometimes in the names of herbs and flowers we find that such a
personification has already taken place (best not to name the herb until
after the exercise).

   In many languages the gender of nouns is already given in the
articles. We speakers of English have to work for it.

   Other suitable subjects for this work are: the colours, the kingdoms
of nature, the four elements (examples can be found elsewhere –
including bringing them into conversation with each other).

But
> *Whose word could be truthful enough
> for the stone to accept it?
> Who could have beauty enough
> to speak for the rose?
> Who could be innocent enough
> to utter what's at the heart
> of a wolf or a goldfish?*

If we attempt to go further with this work of definition two things begin to happen to the language – it veers either towards picture and sculpture, or towards music. That is to say, it is no longer language *about* the subject matter; here it seeks to become identical with its subject.

Language as picture or sculpture

Exercise 75
Write a sentence in hieroglyphics (picture writing) then, ask someone to translate it into English. e.g.

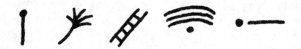

or, write a sentence in English, preferably with some abstractions in it, and ask someone to translate it into hieroglyphics. [see *exercise 234*]

Exercise 76
Resolve the letters of a word into a picture of that word e.g.

or a whole sentence, or a poem as in Apollinaire's 'Calligrams':[36] e.g.

                  D O W N   H E
               E   A
            D   Y   R
            I   M   T
            S
            P   T
            U   H
                                             E

               E   S
               M   A
               A   M
                 L   E
                   F
                  A   A
                     S

[Language as music is dealt with in detail in section 4].

Uttering the inner

Near the beginning of this section of the book [*exercise 13*] we named the random impressions that came to our senses – 'leafless trees .... a cup without a handle.'

Exercise 77
Turn back to them now (or write some others), and then observe the subtle transformation that takes place when we place the words 'I am' in front of them: e.g.

> *I am a cup without a handle*
> *I am the leafless trees*
> *I am three doors*
> *I am the shuffle in the hallway.*

Read them round the group, one sentence per person, as a rhythmic chanting.

Exercise 78
Take one which you find particularly evocative: e.g. 'I am the shuffle in the hallway,' and translate it into adjectives which give the same emotional information – 'shy, hidden, reserved, mysterious', come to mind. Is there agreement in the group?

But now consider the difference in communication between: e.g.

> *I am shy, hidden and mysterious*
> and   *I am the shuffle in the hallway.*

When we first come to creative writing (particularly in adolescence) our feelings are often bound so close to our words that we cannot stand back to consider whether they in fact convey our feelings, however sincere, to the reader. This is not to say that we should never risk our hearts upon the writing (for then we would never come to poetry), but if we label our feelings with emotive adjectives we are only doing half the poet's work. Out of the present exercise a whole language for inner things becomes available.

> Ralph Waldo Emerson: *It is not only words that are emblematic; it is things which are emblematic. Every natural fact is the symbol of some spiritual fact. Every appearance in nature corresponds to some state of the mind, and that state of mind can only be described by presenting that natural appearance as its picture ... the whole of nature is a metaphor for the human mind.*[37]   (from *Nature*)

Exercise 79

Now write a conscious 'I am' piece, finding things in the outer world to interpret you, or not necessarily you but some fictional 'I'. This leaves you freer to play, and holds it on the level of art rather than psychology. e.g.

> *I am the green hill that rolls down to the sea*
> *I am a wrinkle under my mother's eye*
> *I am the wheat-field golden against the sky*
> *I am the call of many seagulls*
> *I am a pink shell on an empty island*
> *I am the white glare of the sun*
> *I am the soft nostrils of a new-born calf*
> *I am the fire-cone as it falls*
> *I am an acorn among the pine needles*
> *I am a blue butterfly in the long grass*
> *I am a red leaf in autumn*
> *I am the sand in the bathroom sink*
> *I am the lamb in the oven*
> *I am the milk that pours.* (Elise Kennedy)

Exercise 80

Bring it into rhyme and metre: e.g.

> *I am the where I have been*
> *I am the more than I mean*
> *I am the hollow horn*
> *I am before I was born*
> *I am I almost forgot*
> *I am a number or not*
> *I am a door closed open*
> *I am a huge word unspoken*
> *I am a nevertheless*
> *I am a no without yes*
> *I am a fisherman's minute*
> *I am a speck without limit.*

Exercise 81

Or with 'I have been ....', which is less naked. e.g.

I have been the sunflower stretching towards the light
I have been the warrior ready to fight
I have been the flame of a bright burning candle

I have been the solid rock hard to handle
I have been the ancient oak-tree in the still grove
I have been the sky turning into mauve
I have been the streaming water boundless and deep
I have been the tumbling stone on the steep
I have been the child oblivious of the day
I have been the sage who grew wiser on his way
I have been the seed impatient to be sown
I have been the fruit the tree of life has grown.

(Marianne Bruszewski)

This takes its inspiration from the Welsh poet Taliesin, whose great 'I have been ...' poem is central to Robert Graves' book, *The White Goddess*.[38]

The ancient stories tell how the Gods spent much of their time shifting their shapes in order to accomplish their designs on Earth – the Greek God Zeus taking swan-form or cloud-form in pursuit of mortal women; and the Norse God Odin, Allfather and God of Poetry, has a multitude of names for his many guises: 'Shifty-eyed, Hooded, Swift in deceit, Truthful, Many-shaped, Changing', are just a few of them.

Those on Earth who wish to take on something of that creative power cannot avoid the shiftiness that accompanies it.

Exercise 82

'I seem to be ..... but really .....' e.g.

I seem to be a lock	*but really I'm a door*
I seem to be a rock	*but really I'm a roar*
I seem to be a groan	*but really I'm a grin*
I seem to be a throne	*that's waiting for a King*
I seem to be a wall	*but really I'm a wave*
I seem to be so small	*but I'm really very brave*
I seem to be a snail	*hiding in its shell*
But really I'm a sail	*that's sailing very well*
I seem to be an ant	*that's feeling rather shy*
But really I'm a planet	*whirling through the sky*
I seem to be a teacher	*good and true and wise*
But really I'm a creature	*telling all these lies.*

Lies, perhaps; but if you are prepared to go deeply enough into this realm of semblance a shift can take place which leads into quite another way of knowing:

Exercise 83
Use the form that we worked with in *exercise 37*, so that the verse can be
read either from the beginning of the line or from the middle: e.g.

> *I am the son of many men*
> *I am the friend of cinnamon*
> *I am the oil in rocks and stones*
> *I am alone with everyone*
> *I gave my gifts of loneliness*
> *I built my house from barrenness*
> *I brought forth life with death*
> *I met with holy breath*
> *I rose to give you life*
> *I live, I am the Son.*
> (Colin Moss)

At this point it should be clear that this is more than a literary exercise.
Starting with play and personal themes it can gradually expand, until
we hear the Cosmic 'I am' speaking. Christ has many such great, 'I
am', sayings, and Krishna, in the *Bhagavad-Gita* names himself in
everything.[39]

In this exploration of natural images as a language for human
inwardness you will certainly find yourself working with some basic
'correspondences':

Weather – a natural image of mood, found in numerous pop-songs –
'it is raining in my heart,' etc. Can you describe your present mood in
terms of the weather? The English are good at this.

Season – mood; also age.

Colour – also mood. Our language is full of such imagery: we feel
blue, see red, go green with envy, sink into a brown study etc..

Flowers – delicate emotions. Ophelia, in *Hamlet*, is well versed in
the language of flowers – 'here's Rue for remembrance' – flower names
themselves often carrying emotional connotations.

Animals – images of deeper, more enduring passions. We know at
once what is being said if someone calls us, 'swine – chicken – wolf –
pig – vixen – bitch – goose – snake.' Why these and not others? It is an
ancient doctrine that in the animal kingdom we find all the qualities of
the human being spread out. [see *exercise 288*]

The four elements – human temperament.

Posture – moral character [see *p. 143*].

In the following poem, translated from the Chinese of Li Po by Ezra Pound, such images are used quite naturally to carry the emotion of the speaker:

THE RIVER-MERCHANT'S WIFE: A LETTER.

While my hair was still cut straight across my forehead
I played about the front gate, pulling flowers.
You came by on bamboo stilts, playing horse,
You walked by my seat, playing with blue plums.
And we went on living in the village of Chokan:
Two small people, without dislike or suspicion.

At fourteen I married my Lord you.
I never laughed, being bashful.
Lowering my head, I looked at the wall.
Called to a thousand times, I never looked back.

At fifteen I stopped scowling,
I desired my dust to be mingled with yours
For ever and for ever and for ever.
Why should I climb the lookout?

At sixteen you departed,
You went into far Ku-to-yen, by the river of swirling eddies,
And you have been gone five months.
The monkeys make sorrowful noise overhead.

You dragged your feet when you went out.
By the gate now, the moss is grown, the different mosses,
Too deep to clear them away!
The leaves fall early this autumn, in wind.

The paired butterflies are already yellow with August
Over the grass in the West garden.
They hurt me. I grow older.
If you are coming down through the narrows of the river Kiang,
Please let me know beforehand,
And I will come out to meet you
                As far as Cho-fu-sa. [40]

The question of how feeling is carried in language will be taken up again in other sections of this book.

An ancient battle

We have seen [*p. 38*] how the poet Coleridge suffered a split between his powerful creative side and the more rational aspect of his nature, which often questioned the validity of his poetic achievement. Eventually that split become so strong that his gift began to fail him. His younger friend, John Keats, was quick to see the cause of it, referring to a quality necessary for poetic creation:

'Negative Capability' – that is when man is capable of being in uncertainties, mysteries, doubts, without any irritable reaching after fact and reason – Coleridge, for instance, would let go by a fine verisimilitude caught from the Penetralium of mystery, from being incapable of remaining content with half-knowledge. [41]

(from a letter)

Elsewhere Keats characterizes the nature of the problem when he says – *What shocks the virtuous philosopher delights the chameleon poet.* [42]

In the case of Coleridge we see the conflict at a time (19th century) when the prevalent rationalism of the culture was just beginning to be challenged by the Romantic poets, who believed so strongly in the truth of the Imagination. To understand it, though, we must go back to a time when the reverse was the case – to Greece in the 6th century B.C., when intellectual thinking was first emerging out of the prevailing mythic consciousness of the ancient world. Plato it was who, speaking of an 'ancient battle between poetry and philosophy,' experienced the tension most keenly in his own soul. Looking back to the earlier poetry of Homer, he says (through the mouth of Socrates):

I have always from my earliest youth had an awe and love of Homer, which even now makes the words falter on my lips … but a man is not to be reverenced more than the truth. [43]

(from *The Republic*, trans. B. Jowett)

He experiences here that the two sides of his nature (his feeling for beauty, and his sense for truth) are being torn in opposite directions.

Plato in his youth had himself been a poet and dramatist, but when he met Socrates he burnt all his earlier writings, denying that poetry was a way to truth. And yet in his later Dialogues he could not escape being both poet and mythmaker.

It is well known that Plato denied a place for poets in his ideal *Republic*:

We must remain firm in our conviction that Hymns to the Gods and praises of famous men are the only poetry that ought to be admitted into our state.

For if you go beyond this and allow the honeyed Muse to enter either in epic or lyric verse, not law and the reason of mankind, which by common consent have ever been deemed best, but pleasure and pain will be rulers in our state.[44]

(trans. B. Jowett)

Three hundred years earlier, however, a poet with that honey on his lips had this to say:

The Muses once taught Hesiod to sing sweet songs while he was shepherding his lambs on Holy Helicon ... "You rustic Shepherds, shame; bellies you are, not men. We know enough to make up lies which are convincing, but we also have a skill, when we've a mind, to tell the truth."[45]

(from *Theogony*, trans. Dorothea Wende)

- and they proceeded to breathe into Hesiod's mouth a sacred voice with which to 'celebrate the things to come and things which were before;' the myths, in fact.

This is a hard saying for 'virtuous philosophers,' to handle. Socrates, asked his opinion of the mythical creatures such as are found in Homer's and Hesiod's stories, says:

I have no leisure at all for such matters, and the cause of it is this – I am not able to know myself. But it appears to me to be ridiculous, while I am still ignorant of this, to busy myself about matters that do not concern me.[46]

(from *Phaedrus*, trans. H. Carey)

With Socrates and Plato we catch the moment in the evolution of consciousness when the old picture language, which communicated directly to the feelings and the will, gave way before the birth of an abstract thinking which could find no inwardness in the ancient stories. Those very stories, however, lamented the coming of such an 'Iron Age', as Hesiod called it, seeing no good in this severance from divine guidance and inspiration. The loss is clear; yet from the viewpoint of the 20th century we can also acknowledge it to be a necessary step towards free thinking and the conscious imagination with which Coleridge was in labour.

Imagination

Coleridge, again: (from *Biographia Literaria*)

It was agreed that my endeavours should be directed to persons and characters supernatural, or at least Romantic; yet so as to transfer from our

*inward nature a human interest and a semblance of truth sufficient to
procure for these shadows of imagination that willing suspension of disbelief
for the moment, which constitutes poetic faith. Mr. Wordsworth, on the
other hand, was to propose to himself as his object, to give the charm of
novelty to things of everyday, and to excite a feeling analogous to the
supernatural, by awakening the mind's attention to the lethargy of custom,
and directing it to the loveliness and the wonders of the world before us.* [47]

This states famously, if a little complicatedly, the two directions of the
Imagination that we have been exploring, i.e.:

- to find the outwardness of inner things (the person objectified).
- to find the inwardness of outer things (the object personified).

Without an understanding of this twofold direction the person of
feeling can find no language for expression, while the person of action
is forever railing against outer injustices, unable to see their inward
causes. Sentimentality and abstraction, propaganda and bombast, are
the result of it.

Our own names

The native American practice of taking names from Nature arises out
of a lively ability to move in the overlap between these worlds. A father
washing his newborn child hears a wolf howling in the darkness, and
when he tells his wife of it she says the child's name is 'Wolf-that-
howls-at-midnight' – apprehending physical and spiritual in one
spontaneous act.

   Some of our English names retain such pictures. 'Jennifer', means
'white wave'. Others (like 'Paul', meaning 'small') are more qualities
than pictures.

Exercise 84
Find out the images and qualities contained in your own names.

Exercise 85
Transform some of your 'I am' sentences into names: e.g. 'Three-
doors', or 'Shuffle-in-the-hallway'. If certain images keep recurring in
your writing then perhaps they come close to naming you, for as Jacob
Boehme says – 'Whatever the Self describes describes the Self'.

Exercise 86
If the members of the group are well-known to each other you can tell

people what flower they are (why do we call people by flower names, but not fruit or vegetables?). Or give each other suitable names from nature. Or Fabulous Names, like *child-of-the-wind-loved-that-bends-the-oak*,[48](Robert Duncan). Or foolish ones: *His intimate friends called him 'Candle-Ends', his enemies, 'Toasted Cheese*.[49] (Lewis Carroll). Or simply write down all the images that arise in connection to a particular person and compose a poem or letter for them drawing upon those images.

Heroes in the ancient world (The Sumerian, Gilgamesh,[50] for example) wanted to leave their names 'stamped on brick', feeling that their eternal destiny depended on it, but now that the Age of Iron has come to an end we can feel our names to be all too stony. John Keats, in the epitaph that he wrote for himself – 'Here lies one whose name is writ on water' – expresses a different possibility. Elsewhere he enlarges on it:

As to the poetical character ... it is not itself – it has no self – it is everything and nothing – It has no character – it enjoys light and shade, it lives in gusto, be it foul or fair, high or low, rich or poor, mean or elevated ... A poet is the most unpoetical of anything in existence; because he has no identity – he is continually informing and filling some other body ...[51]   (from a letter)

Gradually, during the course of this section on statement, the kind of thinking and speaking that we characterized as having an earthy quality has been dissolved, until we come to this watery faculty that can lend itself to anything, daring to live with mysteries, questions and uncertainties.

Three

The Question

QUESTION implies a quest – to find an answer, someone to answer us. Without a question we are forever shut out from the inner life of another. Asking the right question we unlock possibilities of expression in the other. It is the beginning of dialogue.

Exercise 87
Write a list of questions. You could begin each one with a different questioning word: e.g

> *How did you get here?*
> *Can you really trust snowmen?*
> *What colour is Tuesday?*
> *Or should I take up midwifery instead?*
> *Is this your moonmap?*
> *When did you realize the full horror of the situation?*
> *Where have you hidden my puncture outfit?*
> *Who are you anyway?*
> *Will you marry me?*
> *Have you ordered the deathbed?*
> *Which birthmark are you referring to?*
> *Why are you tearing up that bus-ticket?*
> *Do my ears deceive me?*
> *Would you kindly restrain your mongoose?*
> *Shall I show you my X-rays now or after supper?*
> *Did moths make these star-shaped holes in my blanket?*[1]

In coming to the question we leave the firm ground of the statement behind and trust ourselves to the in-betweens, for the question is nothing if not open and receptive. That is the ideal it strives for.

Exercise 88
Write down your basic life-questions: e.g.

> *Who am I?*
> *What is my task in life?*
> *Why am I me and not somebody else?*
> *Is this the right place?*
> *Can we mend the hurts we do to each other?*
> *Why did John Lennon have to die?*
> *Will I be famous?*

Mostly they arise out of our experience of a gap between ourselves and the world, and the need to overcome it. Is it only humans who ask questions? The animals live all the time within the answers that the present moment provides; we, with our memory of the past and our sense of the future, have to work for our answers.

Rainer Maria Rilke:

Be patient towards all that is unsolved in your heart
And try to love the questions themselves.
Do not seek the answers that cannot be given you
Because you would not be able to live them
And the point is to live everything
Live the questions now
Perhaps you will gradually without noticing it
Live along some distant day into the answers.[2]

This is the 'negative capability' [see *p. 60*] that John Keats says is so essential to the poet.

Exercise 89
Approach the place where you are (or a painting, see *exercise 1*) through questions, e.g.

What is this fork doing here in the lamplight? Why is the salt-pot empty? Will the storm stop soon? Have all the oakleaves fallen? Why have they fallen? Where have they fallen? Who owned this table before we did? Did they spread books across it, or only food? Are these books food? How do I know this?

Exercise 90
Play '20 questions' i.e. think of an object (animal, vegetable, mineral – say which) and have the others try to discover it by asking questions. Only yes or no answers can be given. This is such a popular game because it stands so close to the archetype of what questioning is – to unlock the secret which lies hidden in the heart of another, or of the universe.

Exercise 91
Write questions about a particular plant, animal etc.

We are used to asking questions to other people, and questions about the world, but do we ever speak to tables, daffodils, cats, cars? Do they ever answer? Many people would be embarrassed to be caught speaking to a rose-bush, but in the writing group it is necessary to move through that threshold.

Exercise 92

First orally, and then on a paper passed round the group, ask questions to – e.g. a diamond, a clock, a thistle … or to a donkey.

e.g.   *Why do you need long ears?*
       Why submit to all those packs and burdens?
       Why so stubborn?
       Were you wild once before they saddled you?
       Are your long ears only to flick flies away?
       Do you still dream of Jerusalem?
       What are you waiting for?

Exercise 93

Now develop it individually, into a more sustained piece on the same theme. William Blake's poem, 'The Tyger' is a good example, culminating in the marvellous question – 'Did He who made the Lamb make thee?'[3]

Exercise 94

Do the same again, but with the animal, etc., asking the questions [see *exercise 74*].

Wondering

Blake's poem brings us to the questions of origin which awake in young children as soon as they can distinguish themselves from the world – 'Who created God?' – we spend our whole lives trying to answer them. Especially at the edge of sleep such questions arise – 'What is behind the sky?' 'Why does it keep on getting later and later?' They demand a creative answer, not an abstract 'scientific' one.

Exercise 95

Write some origin questions: e.g.

       Why do men have nipples?
       Why can't grass talk?
       Why do fish never smile?
       Why the little dent beneath our noses?
       Why don't snakes have legs?
       Why can beautiful flowers be poisonous?
       Why is taste and talk in the same place?

At this level questioning becomes wondering.

Exercise 96
You could do the same exercise in the form of

I wonder why …

In the book of *Job* we find God overawing Job with such wonders:

> *Then the Lord answered Job out of the Tempest:*
> *Who is this whose ignorant words*
> *cloud my design in darkness?*
> *Brace yourself and stand up like a man;*
> *I will ask questions, and you shall answer.*
> *Where were you when I laid the earth's foundations?*
> *Tell me, if you know and understand.*
> *Who settled its dimensions? Surely you should know.*
> *Who stretched his measuring-line over it?*
> *On what do its supporting pillars rest?*
> *Who set its corner-stone in place*
> *when the morning stars sang together*
> *and all the sons of God shouted aloud?*
>
> *….. Then the Lord said to Job:*
> *Is it for a man who disputes with the Almighty to be stubborn?*
> *Should he that argues with God answer back?*
>
> *And Job answered the Lord:*
> *What reply can I give thee, I who carry no weight?*
> *I put my finger to my lips.*
> *I have spoken once and now will not answer again;*
> *twice have I spoken, and I will do so no more.*[4]

Job cannot answer. Only the child can, or those who have had their 'ancient soul of a child' given back to them – i.e. the poet, the fool, the initiate.

Such an initiate was Enoch:

> *I saw the closed chambers out of which the winds are divided,*
> *the chamber of the mist and of the clouds, and the cloud thereof*
> *hovers over the earth from the beginning of the world. And I*
> *saw the chambers of the sun and the moon, whence they proceed*
> *and whither they come again, and their glorious return.*[5]

Such a child was Piaget's (or anyone's) daughter:

> *Where does that little baby come from? I don't know. Out of the*
> *wood. Are you dust before you are born? Are you nothing at all?*
> *Are you air? Babies don't make themselves, they are air.*
> *Eggshells make themselves in hens. I think they are air too.*
> *Pipes, trees, eggshells, clouds. The door. They don't make*
> *themselves. They have to be made. I think trees make*
> *themselves and suns too. In the sky they can easily make*
> *themselves. How is the sky made? I think they cut it out. It's*
> *been painted.*[6]

Such a fool could be you if you turn to *exercise 131 and exercise 295.*

Questions about questions:

> *What is a conversation?*
> *Can there be a conversation without words?*
> *What is communicated in a conversation without words?*
> *What is communicated in a conversation with words?*
> *Why would one person ask a question of another?*
> *Eliminating selfish reasons, why should one person want to*
> *know the inner state of another?*
> *In what way does it make any difference to a person to be asked*
> *a true question by another person?*
> *Have you ever been asked a true question about your inner state*
> *of being by another person who you felt was inwardly quiet*
> *enough to hear the answer?*
> *If you were asked such a question would you answer it?*
> *Must every true question have an answer?*
> *How can a simple question evoke a difficult answer?*
> *Why would a person talk without being asked a question?*
> *Can a person talk to another, free of selfish reasons, without*
> *being asked a question?*
> *Can a true conversation start without a question?*
> *What is a true conversation?*
> *How does it take place?*   (Greg Richie)

Response ability

So questioning leads to answering – a language coming alive between
you and me – but for that to happen we must first be interested (inter =
between: esse = to be) in each other.

Exercise 97

Why are question marks shaped like that? Give written answers to this question and compare them. It is not for nothing, surely, that the ear is similarly shaped.

Exercise 98

Give a question to your neighbour. When you receive back their written answer observe how it effects you. Are you satisfied? Disappointed? Astonished? Why? e.g.

> *What are all those buttons for?*
> *To keep a close watch on my behaviour.*

Exercise 99

Or write an answer and ask your neighbour to give the question that belongs to it.

Exercise 100

Write one question beginning with the word, 'Why?' Fold it, and pass it on. Now, on the paper you receive, write a 'because' answer without having seen the question: e.g.

> *Why are you blushing?*
> *Because the room is full of poetry.*
>
> *Why were windows invented?*
> *Because a butterfly flew by.*

Again, when you unfold them, notice what happens between question and answer. Perhaps nothing happens. Perhaps the answer is too obvious, too vague, too finished to be interesting. Sometimes, though, you will find yourself answered on a level deeper than you could have imagined; if the answer is not immediately obvious it will set you looking for meanings hidden within the images. That is the point of the exercise – to open the possibility of new levels of dialogue.

Exercise 101

Now try it with – who, when, what, how, which, where (why do so many questions begin with this 'wh' sound?): e.g.

> *Who bit the apple? Your beautiful lame*
>   *daughter.*

When will the leaves turn blue? Yesterday,
  before the tree fell.
What lies beyond the earth? Friendship and
  cleanliness.
How do alligators breathe? By breaking the
  ice.
Which is the most convincing argument? The
  one that doesn't blush.
Where are my bicycle clips? In the space
  between two stars.

This brings us into **Conversation**

'Con-vers-ation' (from the Latin) means 'to turn with' (or, perhaps, to 'make verse together') – 'verse' being found with similar meaning in 're-verse', 'trans-verse', 'ad-verse', and, most beautifully, in 'uni-verse'. That is to say, conversation is a movement and, as such, it can be practised in its essential form prior to language:

Exercise 102

Place your hands against those of an ad-vers-ary and, holding the tension, test each other's forces, turn with each other in a simple wrestling. Let there be a harmonious flow to it to begin with, and then gradually exaggerate the extremes of form and energy, fire and water etc., in a dramatic interchange. Listen to each other with your hands (it can also be done with two wooden rods extending between you). This should not be seen as just symbolic. Observe each other; work with the quality of the conversation. Without a question between you – a basic 'who are you?' – the movement will be completely empty. It needs to be continually recreated out of the space between you. Jacob who wrestled night long with an angel said to him – 'I will not let you go unless you bless me'. The blessing he received (and we all can receive it) was a new name, a new sense of his identity.[7]

Exercise 103

Have a conversation in the group, or with a single partner, by throwing a ball or beanbag between you instead of words. It is the archetypal giving and receiving, questioning and answering. Try to give and to receive it fully, not losing interest, holding attention in a rhythmic turning. Again, it is more than symbolic. It can be practised and observed. Observe the quality of each other's movements. It relates to

how you breathe, and when you get it right you feel your heart goes
with it.

Exercise 104
Then words can be added to the throw – in free association, or as
question – *who, how* etc; as statement – *dog, stone* etc; as command – *go,
stop* etc; as exclamation – *hello, wonderful,* etc. Link the throw to the
breath.

Exercise 105
Play, 'Here we go gathering nuts in May', as a rhythmic wrestling
dialogue. Adults may feel a bit 'silly' at first, but there's nothing wrong
with that.

    Thus, gradually, we can lead the con-versation out of pure
movement towards language, but retaining (hopefully) a sense for
what is moving through our sentences.

Exercise 106
Compose a fairly strict question and answer poem in response to a
partner (the results of *exercise 100* could be a starting point). Nursery
rhymes provide many examples: e.g.

> *How many miles to Babylon?*
> *Threescore and ten.*
> *Can you get there by candlelight?*
> *Yes, and back again.*
> *If your heels are nimble and light,*
> *You can get there by candlelight.*

As an introduction to the task recite such verses as you remember
rhythmically in the group. 'Pussy cat, Pussy cat ...' and 'Mary, Mary,
quite contrary ....' are some other examples. Then, in the writing,
come into a rhythmic dialogue with each other – an exchange of
movement as well as of information; a 'turning together'. It could (but
not necessarily) be in meter and rhyme: e.g.

A. *Which is the way to Paradise Lane.*
B. *First on the left, and then left again.*
A. *When I arrive there what should I do?*
B. *Knock on the door that is painted blue.*
A. *If the blue door opened who would it be?*
B. *If I ran very fast it might be me.*
    But what would you do if I gave you a bone?

A. *I'd tell all the neighbours, the fact must be known.*
B. *And what would you do if I gave you a flower?*
A. *The neighbours and I would build you a tower.*
B. *So why don't you walk down to Paradise Lane?*
A. *Not today, thank you! It's starting to rain.*

(with Pamela James)

As in this example, the one answering can change roles in the middle,
or the questioner can answer with another question.

Here is a more complicated example:

> *Why do grey clouds always cry?*
> *Why do grandmas have to die?*
> *Why do dreams disturb my sleep?*
> *Why do we steal wool from sheep?*
> *Why do stars stay out all night?*
> *Why do soldiers have to fight?*
> *Why do lawyers tell such lies?*
> *Why do blind people have eyes?*
> *Why do we keep cats caged up?*
> *Why do I have to grow up?*

(Lindsay Dearlove)

> *Grey clouds cry for love of Earth.*
> *Grandmas die to find new birth.*
> *Dreams delight us with their charms.*
> *Sheep give wool to keep us warm.*
> *Stars night long spy out the thief.*
> *A soldier fights for his belief.*
> *The lawyer's sorry that he lied.*
> *The blind have eyes to see inside.*
> *The tiger's locked in iron bars*
> *Because we fear his power is ours.*
> *A girl must grow and bring to birth*
> *Courageous love for the lovelorn Earth.*

Exercise 107
Free the conversation now from both the verse form (if you have used
it) and from the alternate questioning and answering. Do not lose the
basic gesture of receptivity, however: e.g.

A. *Listen to the birds!*

B. *Yes, they are quarrelling over a piece of bread.*
A. *I love Robins, but not when they are nasty to each other.*
B. *I love swans. Their nastiness belongs to them.*
A. *What belongs to you and me?*
B. *Only the present moment.*
A. *Then I would like to smell a rose.*
B. *Here is a rose! Don't get lost in it!*
A. *I won't! But the smell makes me think of a friend of mine. Have you got
     a friend?*
B. *I gave it to you, hoping that you would be my friend.*
A. *God bless this present moment! You are this friend of mine!*

(with Bjarne Hjertholm)

It is best to take on a fiction, some imagined circumstance, and speak
to your partner through it. This allows for greater freedom of
expression and, if it becomes too dangerous, you can pretend that
there is nothing to it.

When such dialogues are read out, listen for whether an exchange
has in fact taken place, or whether you have shied away from each
other. The first question and response are often vital in deciding the
level of the whole piece.

Jeopardy

The Troubadours in the South of France in the 12th century played a
literary question and answer game called the 'jeu-parti' –the 'divided
game.' From this comes our word 'jeopardy,' meaning danger. It is a
marvellous root – that in the midst of our word-play we might be
confronted unexpectedly by a real question so that our whole being
stands before a creative risk, a jeopardy, to be faced directly or shied
away from. In the previous piece it happens with the question – 'What
belongs to you and me?', where suddenly the game requires quite
another level of meeting. Such moments in the writing nearly always
have something of the question, 'Who are you?', hidden inside them.
Without that fundamental question, in fact, no real conversation is
possible, and yet we spend so much of our lives talking about other
things in order to avoid it.

When, however, that question is faced the possibility of a poetry
arises:

BALLAD OF THE LITTLE SQUARE

The Children sing in the quiet night: Clear stream, serene fountain!
The Children: *What does your divine rejoicing heart hold?*
Myself: A ringing of bells lost in the mist.
The Children: *You leave us singing in the little square. Clear stream, serene fountain! What do you hold in your vernal hands?*
Myself: A Rose of blood and a white lily.
The Children: *Dip them in the water of the antique song. Clear stream, serene fountain! What do you feel in your mouth scarlet and thirsting?*
Myself: The taste of the bones of my big skull!
The Children: *Drink the tranquil water of the antique song. Clear stream, serene fountain! Why do you go so far from the little square?*
Myself: I go in search of magicians and princesses!
The Children: *Who showed you the path of the poets?*
Myself: The fountain and the stream of the antique song.
The Children: *Do you go far, very far, from the sea and the earth?*
Myself: My heart of silk is filled with lights, with lost bells, with lilies, and with bees, and I will go very far, farther than those hills, farther than the seas, close to the stars, to ask Christ the Lord to give me back my ancient soul of a child, mellowed with legends, with the feathered cap, and the wooden sword.
The Children: *You leave us singing in the little square, clear stream, serene fountain!*
Enormous pupils of parched fronds, wounded by the wind, weep dead leaves. [8]

(Federico Garcia Lorca, trans. J. L. Gili)

Lorca begins by placing us imaginatively in the Square. Then, from the children, comes a powerful version of the 'Who are you?' question: 'What does your divine rejoicing heart hold?' But it is not rejoicing; it has lost the state of childhood. The poet (or whoever 'myself' is) is facing death, or has experienced the death of the child in him, and is now locked into the bones of his 'big skull'. He is aware of it however, and is on a path – the path of the poets – to find imagination consciously – 'my ancient soul of a child,' he calls it.

'Who showed you the path of the poets?' – this question is central to our work together, the main task and possibility of group-work with language being to show each other that path and to give each other permission to step out on it.

'The fountain and the stream of the antique song', is the answer that Lorca gives – it is our answer too: the stream of the poetic tradition, and the fountain of inspiration that can burst out of the ground at any moment. Maybe the group leader (if there is one) consciously assumes the role of being a guide on that path, the initiator, but gradually the whole group can take it on, so that one moment you are the teacher, another moment you are the one being initiated. By asking the right questions we permit each other to enter the imaginative life. You can observe it taking place in the following piece:

Exercise 108

Have a written conversation with a partner in an imagined place [see *exercise 35*].

A. *Can you hear the mice?*
B. *They seem to be feasting in our larder.*
A. *They carry back their crumbs to their children under the floorboards.*
B. *The mere thought of taking any action makes me sick.*
A. *They have little chairs and tables.*
B. *You think technology has entered their lives too?*
A. *Just simple carpentry.*
B. *How lucky they are, being surrounded by the smell of wood!*
A. *What cosy beds they have among the shavings!*
B. *I see I must get out of city stink and concrete.*
A. *And live by imagination alone? Do you believe all this?*
B. *I wish I could, and thus be somewhat truer to myself.*
A. *In Mouse-Town you could be the Town-Cryer, a seller of broadsheets.*
B. *And what a job! – To hawk the latest news – to tell of fire in the sky, of calves born with two heads – in brief, to make my audience stand in awe.*
A. *Fire in the sky! Where? Where?*
B. *Just look and watch and be aware what's happening in the skies.*
A. *I'm so excited!*

(with Elizabeth Long)

Previously, [*exercise 54*] we attempted to characterize things from the mineral, plant and animal kingdoms, and also general subjects, like poets and grandmothers, from the human realm. Now, out of the question 'Who are you?' we can turn to characterize particular human beings:

Exercise 109
Find the portrait of a human being, e.g. the central figure in the Bosch
painting [*p. 9*] and write a characterization of that person.

Exercise 110
Having explored who that person is, step into the picture and become that
person, asking a partner (outside the picture) to engage you in a written
conversation. Try to find the voice that belongs to the character.

There are many ways to do this: e.g.

If there are two characters in the picture you can bring them into
conversation.
You can develop a conversation between a figure in the painting and
the artist.
You can develop characters without any painting there to help you.

When imagined characters start to come alive we reach the beginnings
of drama, the novel, the short-story, where it is all important that the
characters be allowed to evolve their own destinies.

Letters

Some of the early novels in England were composed entirely in the
form of letters written by the various characters. Sometimes as a
literary device it becomes rather awkward, yet it has the virtue of
giving immediacy to the writing, the characters being fully present in
their language.
    The letter is a most powerful form; it can often free you into poetry,
for language becomes real when real people (even if imagined) are
addressed. That is why love poems and poems to God are so powerful,
whereas wise literary statements addressed generally to humanity so
often lack vigour.

Exercise 111
Write a fictional letter to someone in the group and have them write a
reply to it:

Dear Malcolm,

*Well, I did find the church – not on top of a hill as most of the old churches
here in England – but tucked down in a hollow and surrounded by ancient*

appletrees. And so heavy with apples they were that the boughs were almost breaking. I went alone. Freddie wasn't able to come – and I'm half glad, because I was all choked up with emotion and could not have shared it with him. Anyway, with my heart in my mouth, I pushed open the church door and tiptoed in, hoping no one would be about. An old woman was arranging flowers on the altar, but she only smiled politely to me and soon hurried away. I was alone at last, in the place we have thought about so long, Malcolm, and never visited. How I wished then that you were with me in that place of our fathers and our father's fathers. Because it's true. Indeed we have our roots here. The writing on the gravestones is barely visible now, having been worn by the feet of many thousand worshippers. But somehow the sunlight guided me. It was shining through the stained glass window, and throwing a rosy light onto the floor a little to the left of the altar. Yes, I mean it, Malcolm, surely I was guided. For there, worn, but clearly legible, was the name of our illustrious ancestor – 'Lord Grenville, whose mortal remains....' and then the inscription breaks off. But it was enough. The family tradition is confirmed. We are of noble blood, Malcolm, and even though we have fallen into penurious times – let none of us forget it. Do tell mother – it will gladden her last days.

Your loving sister,
Dorothy.

Dearest Sister,

Your wonderful letter did gladden my heart as you can well imagine. For so long we had dreamt about our royal destiny. Do you not remember our pretend castle in the gazebo where I would play Lord Grenville the Fourteenth and you my beautiful and wealthy cousin? Remember that old black suit with the red velvet collar that father let me wear then? He told me that it belonged to his grand uncle, Lucas Grenville, and I felt so proud wearing it, especially next to you in that dress of mother's that was obviously five sizes too big for you. When I think of it, I find it utterly hilarious, but one of my fondest memories. And now to think that it was not really pretend after all. I somehow hold my head a bit higher. I don't dare mention anything of it to the fellows down at the shop, yet they seem to have noticed that I speak up with more assurance at our weekly meetings, and they listen to me more carefully. Susan and the children are absolutely thrilled. I cautioned the children to hold their tongues in the school yard lest jealousy on the part of their schoolmates get the best of them. As you might guess, mother was especially touched. I tried to tell her gently, but the news was just too much for her really. For the past week, she's been taken to her bed and really

*only comes out of her room for afternoon tea. I hadn't realized that it meant
so much to her. I can hear her muttering father's name over and over again
until I fairly well expect that he will answer her in return.*
*Well, I must get on with my duties around the house inspite of our nobility.
Give Walter, Freddie, and the boys my fondest regards.*

> Your brother,
> Malcolm.

(Barbara Hollander)

You can challenge your partner by addressing them as a member of the
opposite sex, for instance – someone quite different from their normal
character. Try to suit the language to the various characters that arise
and, in doing so, take the opportunity to write bad English, cliches,
sentimentalities, etc – all the things you normally forbid yourself to do
in your writing. It is such an open form. You can imply things that
have happened before; you can jump from subject to subject; you can
quote. Anything belongs if it belongs to the character that you have
chosen. Even though you take on a fiction try to speak to your partner
through it – i.e. keep the 'Who are you?' question alive between you.

Exercise 112
You can work with this even more starkly if you write a non-fictional
letter to someone in the group.

Exercise 113
Write a letter to yourself.
    Taken just a little further, this could become the beginning of a
private journal. People often address their journals as 'Dear Diary
.....,' a useful way of getting to know who you are. Share in the group,
if you dare, extracts from your private letters and journals.
    Allen Ginsberg, (in his notes to *Howl, and Other Poems*) said – *I
thought I wouldn't write a poem, but just write what I wanted to without
fear, let my imagination go, open secrecy – something I wouldn't be able to
show anybody, write for my own soul's ear and a few other golden ears.*[9]
    The success of the writing group ultimately depends upon whether
you can develop such 'golden ears' for each other.

The Divided Game

Collaborative writing in general can be regarded as con-vers-ational in that it arises out of a questioning attitude towards a partner or the group. For this reason it is an excellent way of warming people to each other during their first meetings, or for kindling the creative fire at the beginning of any group session before getting down to more serious individual work. Many examples are to be found (as specific craft exercises) throughout this book. Here they are presented for their social and playful aspects.

Exercise 114
Write 'a one word poem', or 'your favourite word', or simply, 'one word'. Introduce the words to each other (orally) by conducting the group – i.e. whoever you point to (however many times) should speak their word. Listen for what happens between the words.

Exercise 115
Write a two word poem, using any two of the words given in the previous exercise. Put them together in the order that is most satisfying to you. Read them round the group, listening again for relationships between the two-word poems. Afterwards you can ask why people chose to put those two words together – what was satisfying about the combination? Even in two words the poetic satisfactions of image, sound and rhythm make their appearance.

Exercise 116
In groups of three, pass round two sheets of paper, each person adding one word to the growing pieces of writing as the papers move past. You may not punctuate after your own word, but the next person may before adding their own word. The exercise centres you on the question – where does the right next word come from in the writing? It also requires an openness for what is emerging, and a responsibility towards unity of meaning, sound, movement, grammar, etc. Do not try to force in the word 'nightingale' when a simple 'and' is called for. e.g.

- *Looping doves will tune their bones to battle.*
- *Sidelong glances feed lemon to sweet amber horses of Andaluse.*
- *Paradise never widens the gap between the endless love of things and the infinite.*
- *Two stones speak with a mountain. They want to ask where the most fragile piece of glass is to be found.*
- *God is .... or tries to .... even begins (hurling himself blithely through time into abysses). Scirocco banana will placate him.*

— Silently the rushing brush swept along.
Three giants juggled nine worlds into song.
And I, small and wondering, wept colourful throngs.

Before reading them out consider in the small groups which of the two
pieces is the more satisfying, and why?

Exercise 117
Write the first line of a free-verse poem, and then pass the paper to the
next person in the circle. They in turn write a line, continuing from the
previous one, but before they pass it on they fold back the first line so
that only their own is visible. And so it continues round until you
decide to stop. The aim should be to carry some unified mood or
meaning through the poem in spite of the unseen part. Unfold the
poem. If it needs editing, do so. Several papers can circulate at the
same time. e.g.

> *The rain fell lightly,*
> *yet the sun was shining*
> *and the birds were singing,*
> *improvising together,*
> *discovering a meaning and*
> *coming to an understanding*
> *of something I wanted to know.*
> *And something I longed to hear*
> *cried unheard within me,*
> *yet louder, more desperate.*
> *My very heart screamed in pain.*
> *Full of rage and frustration*
> *I burnt inside*
> *and brushed aside*
> *and knocked about*
> *in a blue suede coat.*

After a while of receiving lines always from the same person you will
become aware of their particular tone and style. To make this explicit,
read round the lines of each individual as they appear in the different
poems.

Exercise 118
Write a poem, alternate lines with a partner, this time without folding
it. Try to find one voice between you, obeying what the poem wants
rather than what you want the poem to be: e.g.

A rhyming poem:

The furniture movers came today.
George was eating blueberry tart.
Harry drove the horse and cart
Round the bend and into the night.
He huffed and puffed with all his might.

(Robert Sim and ?)

A free verse poem [see also *p. 147*]:

> *When you start*
> *opening*
> *your hand*
> *one finger at a time*
> *you begin*
> *with the thumb*
> *continuing until*
> *all are outstretched*
> *and your lifeline*
> *glows pink in your palm.*
> *This is the map*
> *of where are you.*
> *Now fold it again.*

(with Lindsay Dearlove)

Read them as one voice, then in two voices so that the responding can be heard. Were you in fact listening and responding to each other? Did you assume different roles? Test this by reading just the lines that you contributed.

Exercise 119

Give five words to a partner, receive five words from your partner – e.g.

radiates	bible
spot	crimson
eyeball	Confucius
anthill	prison
star	king

Now compose, alternately, a ten line poem, using one of the words that you received in each line (the order does not matter) until all have been used. You can find one voice together, or it can be conversational: e.g.

Have you ever seen such stars?
Perhaps with the little Prince, a son of the one King.
From the stars, I think, this world looks like an anthill.
What do the stars look like if you see them from a prison?
If you stare too long through the bars they will burn your
    eyeballs.
Confucius *said that our eyes mirror the universe.*
The stars are so bright tonight! Their beauty is without spot.
Look at the crimson *poppy in the clover.*
True! It, too, radiates *a small beauty.*
Just before it dies pick it and press it in your bible.

(with Solveig Mibus)

[For similar exercises see *exercise 278; exercise 282*]

Exercise 120

For an intense experience of a group creation, ask everyone to draw a
line down the page, like this –

| This side is for writing down whatever is spoken. At a given sign the process begins, and whoever speaks (a word, a phrase, certainly no more than a short sentence) has the words written down by everyone: e.g. *The lizard in my pocket....* | This side is for comments on the process or for writing what you would have said if you had said it. e.g *Typical Richard!* |

Now build, as the Spirit moves you, on what has been spoken.

Afterwards you can underline the parts that you provided. Read it
out again in sequence; then each person read just their own phrases.
You can decide beforehand whether it is a poem, a story, a letter etc.,
or you can leave it quite open. It is best done in a fairly small group.
The attention that is required to do it properly can bring out various
tensions in the group, especially if some people talk too much, or if
others are worried about not being able to say anything. It is worth
persevering in spite of such difficulties.

You may call these 'party-games' if you like, but they involve some
'jeopardies' which need to be taken seriously – the main one being that
we are asked to work with 'chance,' to improvise on the edge of the
unknown without having time to censor our meanings. It cannot be
denied that many beauties of language arise through this way of

working, and so we begin to wonder whether such openness to the universe can be maintained in our individual writing and in our collaboration with the Muses. These exercises are an intense schooling of the ability to live in uncertainties that John Keats valued so highly. In the oral tradition there are many cultural forms which seek to nurture this:

Bragging

Under various names – flyting, tenson, jeopardy – and in various forms, the bragging contest or word-wrestling has a long tradition. In its most immediate aspect we meet it in street repartee: e.g.

> Man (caught with his fly zip undone)
> – *Hey, baby, did you see my big Cadillac with the full tyres ready to roll into action just for you?*

> Woman – *No, but I saw a little grey Volkswaggon with two flat tyres.*[10]

or in the playground:

> *'You're a coward and a pup. I'll tell my big brother on you, and he can lam you with his little finger, and I'll make him do it too.'*
> *'What do I care for your big brother? I've got a brother that's bigger than he is; and, what's more, he can throw him over that fence, too.'*[11]

(from *Tom Sawyer*, Mark Twain)

Such acts should not be dismissed as merely obscene or trivial. Through being crossed in such a game we awake to our own identity. Such insults often develop into elaborate rigmaroles, regarded by the community as a training ground for speech-skills.

In Ancient Rome we meet it in more stylized form as 'Amoebian Singing' in which one singer starts with a few lines on a chosen theme. Thereupon his rival improvises some lines in response, outdoing or refuting the previous lines. And so it continues.

Examples can be found in the *Eclogues* of Virgil, where it is expressly said that, 'Alternate song delights the Muses'.[12] Some of them even conclude as riddle contests [*see p. 90*].

In Charlemagne's court it is known as the 'Gaber':

*On their visit to the Emperor at Constantinople Charlemagne and his twelve
paladins find twelve couches made ready after a meal, upon which, at
Charlemagne's suggestion, they hold a Gaber before going to sleep. He
himself gives the lead. Next comes Roland, who accepts willingly, saying,
'Let King Hugo lend me his horn and I will stand outside the town and blow
so hard that the gates will fly off their hinges. And if the King attacks me I
will spin him round so fast that his ermine cloak will vanish and his
moustache catch fire!*[13]

(from Homo Ludens, John Huizinga)

Then another takes his turn.

In Ancient Greece such practices became highly refined in the 'agon'
(contest) between prot*agon*ist and ant*agon*ist in the Chorus of the dramas.

Exercise 121

Engage (in writing) in a lying, boasting, exaggerating, bragging
contest with a partner, outdoing whatever comes before. It is
important to hold it on the level of dramatic tension rather than
personal insult. (It is best introduced through *exercise 42*, with
everyone writing a bunch of lies): e.g.

A. *Yesterday I saw a daisy crying.*
B. *That's nothing. Yesterday I saw a rose and a tulip laughing.*
A. *Oh Yes? Well, the daisy was crying because she knew I saw the tulip
   and the rose blend their colours together.*
B. *Well, I made the rose and the tulip blend their colours together, and that
   made the daisy cry, which I knew was happening, so I didn't look.*
A. *I always look at everything.*
B. *I make everything visible.*
A. *I make everything invisible.*
B. *But I can see all things that are invisible.*
A. *I can look at a blank sheet of paper and see the whole world.*
B. *I can look at a blank sheet of paper and see the whole world, and
   Jupiter, and Mars too, and the moon.*
A. *I can not only see the whole universe in the blink of an eye but I also love it.*
B. *That's nothing. I can see the whole universe, and the other three
   universes, in half a blink and love and hate it at the same time.*
A. *I can see and love and actually be everywhere that ever existed in the
   whole of Infinity.*
B. *I am Infinity.*
A. *I am God.*
B. *I am your mother.*   (Philippa Williams-Brett, Bruce Nichols)

As poets we need the energy that such a dramatic tension can generate. If we ascribe it to ourselves, however, we are in jeopardy of that Luciferic temptation to hurl the Creator out of heaven.

Exercise 122
Some people experience bragging as too masculine an act altogether, in which case do it as a fictional gossip, or as silly talk, outdoing each other with surreal images: e.g.

A. *Mr. Foamy Guinness, when some tables ran out of the backpack the others were left behind.*
B. *But Mrs. Baguettebiscuit, if you would stop flicking elephants off your shoulders, you'd see the artichokes sliding up your chair.*
A. *I don't agree with that. Those shoelaces never reached so far.*
B. *But everyone knows you don't make binoculars out of flea horns.*
A. *Well, when I walked into the corner of the round room all the grasshoppers were awfully offended.*
B. *Then you know why the lightswitch was crying.*
A. *The wheels jumped six times before they were eaten, and this happened 62 minutes before 12.00*
B. *That was after the typewriter kissed the pinecone under the eclipse.*
A. *When I saw that I nearly leaned out of the barbeque table.*
B. *Now the anvils fall from my eyes and I smell moonlight at last.*

(Lotta Gunarsson, George Riley)

This can be taken further into made-up language and name-slinging. [see *exercise 171*]

The people of ancient Europe felt that bragging had something divine about it, Bragdi being one of the Gods who inspired their poetry.

When the hero, Beowulf, arrives at the hall of King Hrothgar he is taunted by Unferth (Strife), who sits at the King's feet, that maybe he is not really the hero he makes himself out to be. At this, Beowulf launches into a great boast about his exploits. Ultimately his boast is that he will kill the monster, Grendel, who is troubling the people. It is clear in the poem that by making his boast he actually takes upon himself the superhuman power to perform the deed.[14]

The role of Unferth in the Beowulf story is an almost ceremonious one, like that of the King's Jester in later times. In the writing group we need to enact that role for each other, for by setting up such a strife, or dramatic tension, a tremendous 'gusto', as Keats called it ('be it foul

or fair, high or low, rich or poor, mean or elevated'), can be released
into the language.

Contraries

Exercise 123
Play 'Good news, bad news', orally round the circle – e.g.

- *The good news is that this is the best book ever written.*
- *The bad news is that nobody can afford to buy it.*
  But the good news is .....

Exercise 124
A fine surrealist game is to write a line and pass it on to the next person
in the circle asking them to write the opposite. When they have done
that they in turn pass it on with only their line showing. And so it
continues, each person writing the opposite. e.g.

> *Close your eyes and jump.*
> *Open your heart and stand still.*
> *Close your mind and keep moving.*
> *Watch out for dead ends.*
> *There should always be one step forwards.*

Exercise 125
Write a list of opposites:

e.g. *light*   *dark*
      remember   *forget*
      closed   *open*

Exercise 126
Pass one pair of opposites to your neighbour and ask them to write the
word that belongs between them:

e.g. *dark*   -   **sunset**   -   *light*
      in   -   **threshold**   -   *out*
      rich   -   **Robin Hood**   -   *poor*
      man   -   **baby**   -   *woman*

Out of such meetings creative activity arises. William Blake was well
aware of this, for in his book, *The Marriage of Heaven and Hell,* he writes –

Without contraries no progression. Attraction and Repulsion, Reason and Energy, Love and Hate, are necessary to Human existence.[15]

Exercise 127

Write, with a partner, or by yourself, a conversation between opposites, taking extreme positions at first and then working towards reconciliation. Take on a voice suited to the quality you have chosen: e.g.

A. *I am your friend.*
B. *That is why I hate you.*
A. *You are my enemy.*
B. *Yes, but I won't tell the reason.*
A. *The Bible says, 'Love your enemies'.*
B. *It's a misprint for, 'Hate your friends'.*
A. *Dear enemy, I love you.*
B. *Dear friend, I dislike you.*
A. *Then why do you call me dear?*
B. *It was a dear with a sneer in it.*
A. *I believe your sneer has a tear in it.*
   What is the reason?
B. *Enemies don't give their reasons.*
A. *Please forgive me if I caused your tears.*
B. *The tears you caused me give me good reason to hate you.*
A. *How did I cause them?*
B. *By loving me too much. If you were a true friend you would keep your love to yourself.*
A. *If I kept my love to myself I would begin to hate myself.*
B. *If you hated yourself you might begin to understand me.*
A. *If I began to understand you perhaps you would make friends with yourself.*
B. *If I made friends with myself you and I would be almost the same person.*
A. *I really must stop talking to myself.*

One of Rudolf Steiner's most helpful insights is related to these creative dynamics. Usually we make simple contrasts between brave and cowardly, beautiful and ugly, good and evil, but Steiner insisted that evil in fact has a twofold nature, and that the good is a dynamic holding of the centre – e.g.

foolhardy	–	**courageous**	–	cowardly
inquisitive	–	**interested**	–	indifferent
infatuation	–	**love**	–	hate

The qualities in the left-hand column he related to the 'Luciferic' temptation of pride, with the tendency to disdain all earthly realities, whereas the qualities in the right-hand column, with their tendency towards contraction, he called the 'Ahrimanic' pole. Only by holding a living balance between them (as Adam does in Blake's painting) can their necessary energies be made fruitful.[16]

We have, actually, been working with a number of such polarities – for instance, the dynamic relationship in language between expression and communication [*p. 42*]. We have also spoken of the need to develop 'negative capability' – i.e. the ability to live in half-truths and uncertainties. Without balancing this, however, with the positive capability of craft and clarity of thinking, Lucifer could easily take hold of it and turn Imagination towards glamour and illusion. Craft by itself would have the opposite tendency and become empty pedantry. As we have seen [*p. 60*] it is a constant battle that poets have to wage within themselves.

Riddles

Another form of the word-contest can be found in Tolkien's book, *The Hobbit*. In the chapter called 'Riddles in the Dark' Bilbo Baggins, lost in the middle of a mountain, challenges the monster Golem to a riddle contest. It is agreed that if Golem loses then he will show Bilbo the way out of the mountain, and if Bilbo loses then Golem can eat him. At this point Tolkien says: *the riddle game was sacred and of immense antiquity, and even wicked creatures were afraid to cheat when they played it.*[17]

Exercise 128
Ask each other some riddles. A well-known one that Tolkien uses is:

> *Thirty white horses*
> *On a red hill.*
> *First they champ*
> *Then they stamp*
> *Then they stand still.* (Teeth)

Exercise 129
Compose some similar verse riddles and begin to engage in the riddle game: e.g.

> *White blameless*
> *Waiting nameless*
> *Without margin*
> *Square Virgin.* (A blank page)

> *A copper King and a silver Queen*
> *jingle in the dark.* (Coins)

A good introduction to this would be to transform your 'moon' metaphors [*exercise 69*] into riddles.

Another good source for riddles is the *Oxford Nursery Rhyme Book*:[18] e.g.

> *The King of Cumberland*
> *Gave the Queen of Northumberland*
> *A bottomless vessel*
> *To put flesh and blood in.*

Children love to make riddle collections, and even come to believe that they themselves composed them, when in fact many have been handed down through generations. But there is no deceit about it. Just as with the words they learn, so the riddles they pick up come without copyright attached.

What the King gave to the Queen was a *ring*. Aristotle says that 'a riddle is a kind of metaphor'[19] [see *p. 49*], and that certainly is the case with the examples given so far. Well, really it is half a metaphor, and we are asked to provide the other half. 'And the greatest thing', says Aristotle, 'is to be a master of metaphor. It implies intuitive perception.' In creating and answering riddles, therefore, we are discerning relationships, correspondences between things and awakening to mysteries. This 'ring' riddle, for instance, is not just a clever comparison; our perception of what a ring means is permanently enhanced by it.

Try to observe the process you go through when someone asks you a riddle. Logic may be part of it, but the answer comes in a flash, an act of 'intuitive perception.' The riddle is an exercise in such perception. It wills us to participate in the act of creation.

For us a riddle is what we find on lollipop sticks. For the old Norse people it was a way of experiencing the world, their names for common things often being in the form of a riddle, or *Kenning:* e.g.

> *Sea = whale path; Body = bone house;*
> *Harp = mirth wood; Sun = world candle;*

Arm = Hawk's land; Bracelet = hawk's land flame;
Poetry = weather-maker's mind strand.

A whole book of their Epic – *The Elder Edda* – is given over to a name-duel between Thor and the dwarf Alvis: e.g.

What is earth called, the outstretched land
In all the worlds that are?

Earth *by men*, The Fold *by gods*,
Vanes call it The Ways,
Giants Evergreen, *elves* Growing,
High gods call it Clay.

What is the moon called, that men see
In all the worlds that are?

Moon *by men*, The Ball *by gods*,
The Whirling Wheel *in Hel*,
The Speeder *by giants*, The Bright One *by dwarves*,
By elves Tally of Years.[20]

(trans. Paul B. Taylor and W. H. Auden)

Exercise 130

Give each other similar questions and use the form given here to make up your own Kennings for common things. 'All the worlds that are ......' might include those of the elemental beings mentioned on *page 52*.

Now go and look at the world through elves' eyes – not 'earth' but 'growing', not 'moon' but 'tally-of-years'.

Yes, the riddle game is indeed sacred. There is a suggestion that the *Edda* actually consists of fragments of a ritual, performed not as entertainment but as a naming of Creation in order to hold it together. It tells how the God Odin visits the giant Mimir and how, in return for one of his eyes, receives a draught from the Spring of Wisdom. To test his new powers Odin challenges Vafthrudnir, wisest of all the giants, to a riddle contest. They ask each other about the secrets of world creation (questions, again, which only the initiated can answer) –

Vouch to me first, Vafthrudnir,
If your wisdom serves you well:
How did the earth, how did the sky
Both of them come to be?
From Ymir's flesh was earth shaped,

> *The mountains from his mighty bones,*
> *From the skull of Frost Cold was the sky made,*
> *The Salt sea from his blood.*[21]
>
> (trans. Paul B. Taylor and W. H. Auden)

Finally Odin wins by asking what Odin will whisper in the ear of his
dead son Baldur. The giant cannot answer, and so forfeits his life.

Exercise 131

Try, in one sentence, to answer the greatest riddle of all: What was it
like before the world began? e.g.

> *Beyond the beyond*
> *Before the before*
> *Nobody knocked*
> *On nobody's door.*

[for an extended version of this see *exercise 295*].

Whatever your answer it cannot be other than a metaphor.

A riddle is more than a metaphor, however. In the old Anglo-Saxon
riddlebook the riddler enters into a thing and asks not 'What is it?' but
'Who am I?' e.g.

> *I was in one hour an ashen crone*
> *a fair-faced man, a fresh girl,*
> *floated on foam, flew with birds,*
> *under the wave dived, dead among fish,*
> *and walked upon land a living soul.*[22]
>
> (trans. Michael Alexander)

Unfortunately the answer has not come down to us.

Exercise 132

Compose a 'Who am I?' riddle: e.g.

> *I shed my blood*
> *To show your mind.*
> *My blood is black*
> *And underlined - who am I?*
> (Pen)
>
> *Leonardo dyed my hair,*
> *Picked me up by the tail –*
> *Mona Lisa was there – who am I?*
> (Paintbrush)

At its deepest level this requires the ability to lend your voice to something other so that it can articulate its own nature. [see *exercise 73*].

Such an ability must have been Adam's when the animals asked, 'Who am I?' and he had to name them [see *p. 22*].

Here is yet another aspect of the riddle – it throws us, with a slight unease, back into that Eden state (the realm of the Un-things, [see *p. 154*]) where everything is nameless. Naturally, children who have so newly come from there delight in the experience that riddling provides of bringing order into chaos through the power of naming.

Exercise 133

Write a one word poem [see *exercise 114*], and then give it a title. The title can be as long as you like: e.g.

> *A small measure of song: Chaffinch.*
> *Morning metal: Kettle.*
> *Little things that defeat us: Mosquitoes.*

Read the title in such a way that it prepares the space to receive the poem.

The old riddling experience is re-appearing in some areas of modern poetry. When Lorca, for instance, ends his poem [*p.76*] with 'enormous pupils of parched fronds wounded by the wind weep dead leaves,' the images are not chosen to illustrate some easily translatable idea. They communicate, and yet we are left questioning. The modern image is a verge at which, calling upon all our powers of 'intuitive perception,' we must ourselves create.

[For an extension of riddles see *exercise 288*]

Jokes

Joke telling, especially among men, is part of the modern social ritual. To grasp a joke requires the same kind of intuition that we observed in the riddle – especially 20th century humour, with its taste for the absurd, bringing together disparate elements; we laugh to resolve the tension.

In the Sufi tradition jokes told about Mullah Nasruddin are also wisdom stories: e.g.

On one occasion a neighbour found Nasruddin down on his knees, looking for something. "What have you lost, Mullah?" "My Key," said Nasruddin. After a few minutes searching, the other asked – "Where did you drop it?" "At home." "Then why, for heaven's sake, are you looking here?" "There is more light here".[23]

(from *The Sufis*, by Idris Shah)

On one level we laugh; on another, taken as meditations, they can bring us into a new way of thinking. Nasruddin is the wise fool – we laugh at him, and then begin to realize that we ourselves are the foolish ones. The joke-telling ritual lives on the edge of such a jeopardy.

So, jokes should not be dismissed as trivial. They are a child's introduction to the intuitive life, and in the writing group laughter has an essential function as safeguard against over-intensity. When asked to read out what they have written people often begin to giggle. This must be accepted as part of the process; it is a sign that the breath is being released, and the heart opening up. The group leader, if there is one, needs to be a master of teasing.

Sacred Dialogue

Such masters are to be found in abundance in the practice of Zen Buddhism, where the joking or paradoxical question becomes a sacred technique in the Koan. e.g.

What is the sound of one hand clapping?

Obviously the pupil cannot answer on a literal level. The question asks for an inner change, a shift in consciousness.

Exercise 134

By adapting the words and form of the well-known song, 'Scarborough Fair,' we can approach such a level of dialogue: e.g.

> *Will you give me an acre of land*
> *Between the sea foam and the sea sand?*
> *If you promise to plough it with a lamb's horn*
> *And sow it all over with one peppercorn.*
> *Will you give me .....*
> *If you promise .....*

It could be made even simpler without the verse form.

In the Ancient Indian tradition the technique is reversed. In this example from the *Upanishads* the pupil comes to question the master:

How many Gods are there, Yajnavalkya?

As many as are mentioned in the Hymn to all the Gods, namely three hundred and three, and three thousand and three.
Yes; but just how many Gods are there, Yajnavalkya?
Thirty-three.
Yes, but just how many Gods are there, Yajnavalkya?
Six.
Yes, but just how many Gods are there, Yajnavalkya?
Two.
Yes, but just how many Gods are there, Yajnavalkya?
One and a half.
Yes, but just how many Gods are there, Yajnavalkya?
One.[24]

At this point the pupil stops asking; he has given birth to the answer that he was already pregnant with.

Socrates, another wiseman, spoke of himself as a midwife who, by asking the right questions, could help the citizens of Athens bring forth the knowledge that was in them. Such a drawing out, or 'educing', is the root of 'education'.

Oracles

In earlier times people who had burning questions went to consult the Oracles, where Sybils speaking in trance, or Soothsayers who could read the quality of the times in the way the birds were flying or the oakleaves rustling (see Blake's picture again), would give their answers – often in a riddling poetic form which called upon the questioner to be inwardly active: e.g.

> Let your magic tortoise go, and look at me
> with the corners of your mouth drooping.[25]
> > (from *I Ching*, trans. Richard Wilhelm)

It was a time when poets were still useful, functioning as priests and guides to the people.

Festivals

Rudolf Steiner (from *The Cycle of the Year*):

Mankind has long ago forgotten why the songbirds sing. It is true that men have preserved the art of song, the art of poetry, but in the age of intellectualism in which the intellect has dominated everything, they have forgotten the connection of singing with the whole universe. ... For when at a certain time of year the larks and the nightingales sing, what is thereby formed streams out into the cosmos, not through the air, but through the ethereal element; it vibrates outward in the cosmos up to a certain boundary ... then it vibrates back again to Earth, to be received by the animal realm – only now the divine-spiritual essence of the cosmos has united with it. ... In those ancient times this was understood, and therefore the pupils of the Mystery-schools were instructed in such singing and dancing as they could then perform at the St. John's festival, if I may call it by the modern name. Human beings sent this out into the cosmos, of course not now in animal form, but in humanized form, as a further development of what the animals send out into cosmic space. – And there is something else yet that belonged to those festivals: not only the dancing, the music, the song, but afterward, the listening. First there was the active performance in the festivals; then the people were directed to listen to what came back to them. For through their dances, their singing, and all that was poetic in their performances, they had sent forth the great questions to the divine spiritual of the cosmos.[26]

True, the oracles have fallen silent, and we find it more and more difficult to celebrate the traditional festivals. But if we can regard the poetry we make, however humble, as an offering sent out on such wings, then moments of festival could enter our daily lives; and if, through a life in poetry, we can develop our faculties of imagination, then everything would speak to us.

German nineteenth century drawing (after Indian original)

Four

The Exclamation

EXCLAMATION is language as direct expression of the inner life –
to clamour, to cry out – its ideal being to sound the heart's tone truly.

So often the voice of our education insists that we withdraw from
exclamation into detached statement and reported speech, where we
talk about our feelings instead of expressing them from the inside.
This is particularly so with the English who (since Bacon, Locke and
Newton established the scientific mode of observation) have cultivated
the stiff upper lip and lack of involvement. In the 18th century one of
our finest poets, Christopher Smart, even had to be locked up on
account of his enthusiasm for praising the Lord in public. There was
no stopping him, however, for in his 'Jubilate Agno' the praise kept
pouring out. This attitude of praise (as he says there) 'can give to a
mute fish the notes of a nightingale.' No doubt he was ill; but on the
other hand you can become ill by having your joys and woes locked up
inside you.

Exercise 135
So, take permission here to write down all the exclamatory noises,
words and phrases that you know – old fashioned ones, ones you are
afraid of – and then exclaim them round the group.

Exercise 136
Write some exclamatory sentences and consider what makes them so:
e.g.

> *What a wonderful day!*

In this example the exclamation comes to fullest expression in the
adjective 'wonderful'. Often a single adjective – e.g. 'marvellous' or
'disgusting' – cried out with vigour, is sufficient for giving utterance to
what lives inside us. It is true that adjectives can seriously clog up a
piece of writing, labelling emotions rather than conveying them, but
such outpourings should not be inhibited in the group. Often a fine
piece of poetry lives on the edge of banality or sentimentality – e.g.

> *Alone, alone, all all alone,*
> *Alone on a wide wide sea.*[1]

Yet if Coleridge had written, 'all alone on a wide sea,' instead, how
much poorer it would have sounded. Once the energy of feeling is
flowing it can, if necessary, be shaped and crafted. Without it we are
left with only artifice and literary devices.

Exercise 137
Approach the place where you are (or a painting [see *exercise 1*]) through exclamation. Indulge the adjectives: e.g.

> *How windy it is tonight! What a comforting light this lamp casts! And yet how small it is! And such an endless universe! The grain of this table is very beautiful!*

As an exercise this is difficult, for unless it comes out of real feeling the language will be stilted.

Exercise 138
Write a praise or a boast for some thing, animal, or person that you feel close to: e.g.

> *Praise to the Rooster who praises himself.*
> *He makes no use of understatement.*
> *Praise to his red comb and fiery tail.*
> *The divine spark is in them.*
> *Praise to his lack of doubt.*
> *Praise to his holy shout.*
> *Call out to the awakeness in us all,*
>   *O Rooster!*

Exercise 139
Or a praise addressed directly to the object or person.

Exercise 140
Or where the object exclaims itself.

Praise is one of the chief offices of the poet. Caedmon, as we have seen [*p. 3*] was commissioned by an Angel to 'sing the creation,' and the German poet Rainer Maria Rilke saw it as his task to 'praise this world to the Angel,' and thereby to transform it.[2]

Lament is another of the poet's official duties. In writing groups people are often so apologetic about their poems before reading them out that it might be good to go the whole hog –

Exercise 141
Write an apology – for your poetry, for your character, behaviour, existence, whatever; or an apology to the earth, etc.

This as an archetypal act becomes the ritual of confession leading to absolution.

Among the first poets to give lyrical expression to personal feeling
was King David. In his Psalms these acts of praise and lament are
magnificently embodied.

Exercise 142
Write a 'Please' poem. This leads towards prayer.

Exercise 143
Write a 'thank you' poem. This leads us to graces [*exercise 218*].
If these are given as tasks in the group they can be suited to the
different temperaments of those present.

Exercise 144
Write a wish poem. This can be done collaboratively, each adding a
line as a paper is passed round: e.g.

> A wish for fishes –

> *I wish you to be sleek and slender.*
> *I wish you to understand profundity.*
> *I wish you to carry light in your tails*
> *into obscurities where no brightness comes.*
> *I wish you to people the deep.*
> *I wish you to be the clappers of the bells*
> *in all the drowned steeples.*
> *I wish you to speak the word at last*
> *that you are always mouthing.*
> *I wish finness to your fins.*

or   A fish wish –

> *I wish God had stopped on the 5th day.*
> *I wish to be the fish I am.*
> *I wish my eyes could meet the eyes of others.*
> *I wish I could tell the difference*
> *between my tears and the sea.*

Exercise 145
They could also be wishes for yourself, a playful way into it being to
fold the paper between each line: e.g.

> *I wish I were the wild west wind*
> > *drinking my tea*
> > *on the tip of a giant's finger.*

All these wishes have been exclamations, but it could move towards the command – i.e. language not just expressing feeling, but attempting to make something happen [see *exercise 219*].

Exclamation does not only take the form of words and articulated sentences. It is present whenever people 'jump for joy' and start waving their arms about; and when 'out of heart's abundance the mouth speaketh' its first expression is often the single vowel or syllable, or (more primary still) the gasp or sigh. HWAET! is how the Saxon poem 'Beowulf' begins – no word at all, but the first releasing of the breath after inspiration. It seems a mixture of the 'how' and the 'what' which precedes many of our modern exclamations.

Exercise 146
These gestures, and this release of the breath can be enhanced by practising that childhood activity of skipping – just skipping along; or with a skipping rope, perhaps accompanied by one of the many traditional skipping rhymes such as –

> *Pease porridge hot, pease porridge cold,*
> *Pease porridge in the pot, nine days old.*
> *Some like it hot, some like it cold,*
> *Some like it in the pot, nine days old.*

Exercise 147
Discus throwing also belongs here. This can be done very simply, with a beanbag or even with an imaginary discus. The important aspect is that, after a preparatory spiralling in and out, the discus (and the breath) is released and that the eyes and whole expression of the face follow the flight of it.

Once that breath is moving, we shape it (whether spontaneously or conventionally) into vowels and sounds which accord with our mood and feeling. Even when (clothing our emotions in meaningful words) we cry, '*What a wonderful day!*' it rises to a height in the syllable 'won' which is more of a 'wow' than a word here. It is the sounds and intonations of the language which carry so much of its feeling content – how else could we be so deeply moved by poetry in a language that we do not 'understand'?

In previous exercises we have not been unaware of this pre-dictionary level of the language, but in this section we will give it special attention. Having said this, it must also be said that it is difficult to work consciously with word-music – it can so easily become a mere cleverness with noises, rather than a revelation of what the heart holds. Clearly some people are born with a better ear for language than others. If you are not one of them don't be discouraged. The ear can be trained, primarily by learning good poetry by heart, including your own, and speaking it aloud. If this embarrasses you you should train your dog, as William Wordsworth did, to warn you when someone is coming.

Noises

Exercise 148
Drop an object. Write down exactly the noise it makes: e.g.

> *Nudcge*   –   (a falling pencilcase)
> *Pumpf*   –   (also a pencilcase)
> *Icg*   –   (a glass against the table)
> *Pink*   –   (a leaf falling on a table)

Exercise 149
Drop another object. 'Crash', 'boom,' 'bang,' etc. – which comes the closest? Is there any agreement in the group? Unlikely – for it soon becomes clear that inanimate objects do not use vowels and consonants, though they approximate.

Exercise 150
Consider what animals say. Do cuckoos really speak their names? Do cows really moo? (Dutch cows say 'boo'). German dogs say 'Vou, Vou'.

Exercise 151
Show someone a sunset. What noise do they exclaim? Or stamp on somebody's toe. Do they say 'ow' in China? The English, of course, say nothing. Well, maybe they say 'Sorry'.

We are exploring here whether certain vowels naturally express certain emotions. You can experiment with this. And when the pencilcase says 'nudcge' is it exclaiming itself? Is the Donkey?

Rudolf Steiner (on the origins of language): *They did not yet have language in the true sense. Rather, what they could utter were natural sounds which expressed their sensations, pleasure, joy, pain and so forth, but which did not designate external objects. ....Among women, that which lived within them could transpose itself into a kind of natural language. For the beginnings of language lie in something which is similar to song. The energy of thought was transformed into audible sound. The inner rhythm of nature sounded from the lips of wise women. One gathered around such women and in their songlike sentences felt the utterance of higher powers. …For at that period there can be no question of sense in that which was spoken. Sound, tone, and rhythm were perceived.*[3]

(from *Cosmic Memory*)

Such women were the original gossips, i.e. God-sybils.

Exercise 152

Make up a new word to be sad with – e.g. *oongavool*.
And a word to be happy with – e.g. *alamadinka*.
And a new swear word (a word to be angry with) and then swear it – e.g. *Krimflatox*.
Now say the sad one happily and the happy one sadly. Does the feeling live only in the way you say it? Or does it live partly in the choice and length of sounds?

Exercise 153

Make a list of your ten favourite words. Why do you like them?

Exercise 154

Write a list of onomatopoeic words, where the sounds imitate what is being named – e.g. *cuckoo, crash, grumble* – and then, more subtly, where they do not merely imitate a sound, but correspond to some inner colouring or gesture – e.g. *swollen, glib*.

Exercise 155

Translate *Alone, alone, all all alone,*
             Alone on a wide wide sea

into a language that has never been spoken before. Does it change the emotional content?

New Languages

Exercise 156

Write a few sentences in a completely new language – a unified grammatical language, not a jumble of noises: e.g.

> *Im gromlen den kappen ruck gib rid ooslap. Klam zucker roodle furd ye schlip – nack, om zee yuk yacker gib. Grof im ye*

shleck, om zigger yack flod, zit zee dibble grup, ort zippen ye
nackel. Klob, jee riddle dun dapple-dig.
(Nick Huber)

In this exercise the 'inhibition' of meaning is completely removed. You
are free to choose the next word entirely by ear. It is another important
threshold. Some people, approaching it, have been known to blush all
over, the whole body becoming tuned to another source of meaning.

Read out the results, several times if necessary, until the ear grasps
them. Do they satisfy or not? How do they relate to your normal
writing style? And (though you won't be able to answer) why did you
choose to write with those particular sounds and rhythms? Although it
can be an embarrassing exercise some people find in it a freedom and
seriousness which they ordinarily lack in their writing. Embarrass-
ment (by the way) is closely related to poetry. John Keats tells us that
even the Hippocrene, the fountain of the Muses, is 'blushful'.

Exercise 157

If you now bring the various new languages, orally, into conversation
with each other, it will confirm what was said about feelings being
conveyed through the sounds, rhythms, and intonations of the
language. You might also hear different kinds of beings, different
nationalities speaking to each other, or you might hear only the
'confusion of tongues' that resulted from the fall of the tower of Babel
[see p. 119].

In Dante's *Inferno* we meet Nimrod (the legendary builder of that
tower) babbling incoherently – *Rahel mahee amek zabi almit ....,* and
Dante comments –

> *His very babbling testifies the wrong he did on earth; he is*
> *Nimrod through whose evil Mankind no longer speaks a*
> *common tongue. Waste no words on him; it would be foolish.*
> *To him all speech is meaningless; for his own, which no one*
> *understands, is simply gibberish.*[4]

(trans. John Ciardi)

Or you might hear it as an attempt to speak with tongues, as some
Evangelicals do: e.g.

> *Yah-muh-nug kee-tuh see-yuh-nah-yuh-see ah-nuh-kee-yah-*
> *nuh tee-yah-sah-nah-yah ah-nah-kee-yah-tah-nah see-yuh-*
> *nah-yuh-see*

claiming that is is a divine universal language which can be inter-
preted. The woman from New England who spoke the example given
here, however, never went beyond the sound possibilities offered by
her native language.[5]

The word 'Babel', though it has come to be associated with
confusion, actually means, 'door of God,' pointing towards a serious
level of work within this nonsense.

J.R.R. Tolkien in his book, *The Lord of the Rings*, took it very
seriously, creating new languages suited to the inner nature of the
various beings that inhabit his pages: e.g.

> *A Elboreth Gilthoniel*
> *Silivren Penna Miriel*
> *O Menel aglar elenath!* .....(Elf language)

or from the dark land of Mordor:

> *Ash Nazg durbatulik, ash naz gimbutal,*
> *Ash Nazg thrakutulak agh buzum-ishi*
> *Krimpatul.*[6]

These languages characterize aspects of the elemental beings of nature
who, until recent times, were recognized and respected, and even
addressed, by human beings. Shakespeare includes them sympathet-
ically in his plays. They are known by many names. Here we can
characterize them as

Salamanders:	beings of fire
Sylphs:	beings of air
Undines:	beings of water
Gnomes:	beings of earth

Exercise 158

Create your own new languages to express the qualities of the four
elements and their beings [see *p. 124*]. e.g.

Fire:	*Traff lickiti plaff, taf tiffle blim nimbleshaff*
	shish ashafish nash nizzel. Ziggabrazaggabik.
Air:	*Avliavla van val in wim tith toth lonlioth*
	alwinsom novni lim blithen withwothel.
Water:	*Wa lalla molvu muma la fa allolala awal.*
Earth:	*Frodge braked placks*
	Dobido dacka erdi erbo
	Crod bagaratad.

Try to make conscious which sounds, rhythms, type and shape of sentence, etc., belong to each element. Clap their rhythms.

In group work it is interesting to note how a person's inner element (i.e. temperament) often rebels against the given task, dampening the fire, making earth sparkle. To test your languages ask someone outside the group to guess which element is which.

Exercise 159
Write a paragraph in Russian, or Italian, or any other language that you do not know but which you have a sense for.

Exercise 160
Write a new language in verse form: e.g.

> *Oxtwitch witchet paxtot rose*
> *Ormulu romulu romus nose*
> *Sentchin tenify, tenify sooth-hey*
> *Hoomush gugwash gippig may.*
> *Yap yap ooze knees*
> *Hompom rose please*
> *Ormulu romulu romus nose.*
> *Twitchenim oxtwatt adot nit*
> *Inch ache ounce formulus fit*
> *Adelib addelib, addelib heh-ho*
> *Ooshla eesa tetrog come go.*
> *Grunk grunk ooze kneeze*
> *Feroog rose please*
> *Ormulu romulu romus nose.*
>   (Hilary Kidman)

[for even stricter forms see *p. 159*].

Hugo Ball, one of the founders of the Dadaist movement, wrote:

I invented a new species of verse, 'verse without words,' or sound poems, in which the balancing of vowels is gauged and distributed only to the value of the initial line. The first of these I recited tonight:

> *Gadji beri bimbá*
> *Glandridi lauli lonni cadori*
> *Gadjama bim beri glassala*
> *Glandridi glassala tuffm i zimbrabim*
> *Blassa galassasa tuffm i zimbrabim*

*I now noticed that my voice, which seemed to have no other choice, had
assumed the age-old cadence of the sacerdotal lamentation.*[7]

(trans. Eugene Jolas)

Exercise 161
Write such a piece, determining the mood (e.g. anger, lamentation)
beforehand. Speak what you write in various moods.

As Hugo Ball came to realize, this is not so new really. When
Shakespeare wrote 'with a hey nonny nonny no' at the end of his song,
it is a similar continuation of the feeling after the meaning (whatever
that is) has stopped. Children, with their 'Chinese Counting', have
always known it:

Exercise 162
Recite together in the group –

> *Eenie meenie macka acka*
> *Hi di dominacka*
> *Stickeracka roomeracka*
> *Om pom push.*

Then one line each, passing it on. Then half a line each. Then all
together again, passing your pens around in rhythm.

Exercise 163
Using the same form exactly, compose new words for it.

Exercise 164
Write a sound (noise?) poem, dissolving the grammars entirely. At this
extreme poetry becomes the *cuckoo jug-jug pu-we to-witta-woo* of
Thomas Nash – pure music and birdsong; or the Beast Sound of
Michael McClure:

> *AHH GRHHROOOR! AHH ROOOOH. GARR*
> *nah ooth eeze farewell. Moor droon fahra rahoor*
> *rahoor, rahoor. Thee ahh-oh oh thahrr*
> *noh grooh rahhr.*[8]

Mircea Eliade: *In preparing his trance the Shaman drums, summons his
spirit helpers, speaks a 'secret language', imitating the cries of beasts and
especially the songs of birds. He ends by obtaining a 'second state' that
provides the impetus for linguistic creation and the rhythms of lyric poetry.
Poetic creation still remains an act of perfect spiritual freedom. Poetry re-*

*makes and prolongs language; every poetic language begins by being a secret
language, that is, the creation of a personal universe, of a completely closed
world. The purest poetic act seems to re-create language from an inner
experience that like the ecstasy or religious inspiration of primitives' reveals
the essence of things.*[9]

(from Shamanism: Archaic Techniques of Ecstasy)

Non Sense

The guardians of 'proper English' often put up barriers against 'slang,'
regarding it as language in decay. No doubt that is true to some extent,
but the danger is that this attitude becomes a defense against the re-
creation of language that Eliade is speaking about. In that case the
language becomes static, coffined in dictionaries. The aim of these
exercises is to plunge back for a moment into the 'caverns measureless
to man,' where, according to Coleridge, 'Alph, the sacred river' runs,
ever creating new words and alphabets for poets to make use of.

Exercise 165
The first verse of Lewis Carroll's, 'Jabberwocky' (which you can
imitate) is a famous example of a conscious working with this:

> *Twas brillig, and the slithy toves,*
> *Did gyre and gimble in the wabe,*
> *All mimsy were the borogoves,*
> *And the mome raths outgrabe.* [10]

Exercise 166
Return to some of the pieces you have written and replace the
adjectives, nouns and verbs with made-up words.

It is probably too late to warn you of a dis-ease that poets are liable to
catch – that of making 'spoonerisms' out of anything that is said to
them. 'Style and tone of voice' immediately becomes 'tile and stone of
voice,' or when Bill Jones is introduced he is changed into Jill Bones
without him knowing it.

Exercise 167
Those who have suffered this dis-ease for some time might find some
relief in imitating the following transformation of *Little Red Riding
Hood*: (nobe oddy nose hew row tit):

Wants pawn term, dare worsted ladle gull hoe lift wetter murder inner ladle cordage honour itch offer lodge dock florish. Disc ladle gull orphan worry ladle cluck wetter putty ladle rat hut, end fur disc raisin pimple caulder ladle rat rotten hut. Wan moaning rat rotten hut's murder colder inset: Ladle rat rotten hut, heresy ladle basking winsome burden barter and shirker cockles. Tick disc ladle basking tudor cordage offer groin murder hoe lifts honour udder site offer florist. Shaker lake, dun stopper laundry wrote, end yonder nor sorghum stenches dun stopper torque wet strainers.....[11]

Exercise 168
Read some of your previous writings backwards, either word by word or line by line, to free them a moment from the meanings you imposed on them.

Exercise 169
Write a piece of 'absolute rubbish,' using real English words, but free from their accustomed meanings. It can still be grammatical: e.g.

Shipwreck under my nose, twilight come float jig. Around some dinner smack is given lip roast billet. Fray me come link, oar snap on jerk flipper flap. Ram, and dip this node if thyme jumps saving grip snort. Later up round battle, blasting one din came soft in ripples. Balance time wriggler, smiling sentence or never lost. Cup-riddle, spoon saver, beget giant relief.

(Nick Huber)

Exercise 170
Try it in lyrical form with a predetermined mood – sadness in this case:

Table glaze of a narrow harmony
but a windcat willow not engine trouble.

Ah but oh. And a flute rose trembles.
Flute of a bird bone. Petal feather quivers
alone and growing.

No, but somebody where was hobbled
in skill in sky. Know why I'm catkin.

Bake the true cake. Teeth beneath.

Apple above my love and growing.

Who did. Who. Who did it owl asks.
Whoever white winter bread Friday next
with his ghost in tatters.

Table glaze of a wintry music horn.
I'm sad I'm sorry. Ah but oh.
And a winternox blue cat no it's
not your fault. Flute cracked and wintry.

Even more of a challenge would be to use some of the strict poetic forms found in the next section. [see *p. 159*]

Exercise 171
Or do it in dramatic form, with a bit of name-slinging thrown in: e.g.

A. *You scrodged my book.*
B. *Fishooks!*
A. *Yodshits – just give it back.*
B. *When Ganglia bleed turnips.*
A. *There is no need to be ingruntle bloots … all I flude was you scrodged my book. Frogat Bloo!*
B. *Hyperventilate and ransom all you want, chalk smears and cattle prods.*
A. *You need your crampolia skwonked.*
B. *Crestophile … withered tendrils mar your spigot!*
A. *That's not the point you womping fleepit – my spigot is entirely my own affair. I hope you womp your toe in a skrinka.*
B. *I wouldn't wish that on my worst enemy, you antideluvian crankcase! Besides, assonance will get you nowhere.*
A. *Now let's not get warty about this – you scrodged my book didn't you?*
B. *Yes, but only cynically.*
A. *Cynically! … wadsquits right out the door! Squinkly, more like!*
B. *Squinkly? Battleships! Christened anchors would sink beneath your sludge. Abercrombie and Fitch woman …. you'd sassafrass forever!*
A. *Just you wadge your flippers or I'll grog your winker. Floppy old Goobat. I never sassafrassed you until you gruntleblooted me.*
B. *Oh kettledrum, dragging molten fish from gristled closet is anachronistic. I'm not going to wombat anymore.*
A. *Don't change the subject.*
B. *Take your book and squelch it! Anagrams!*

(Michael Jacobs, Paula Brown)

Thomas Carlyle :

> *All speech, even the commonest speech, has something of song in it: not a parish in the world but has its parish accent – the rhythm or tune to which the people there sing what they have to say. Accent is a kind of chanting; all men have accents of their own – though they only notice that of others. Observe too how all passionate language does of itself become musical. All deep things are song. It seems somehow the very essence of us, Song; as if all the rest were but wrappages and hulls! The primal element of us; of us, and of all things. The Greeks fabled Sphere-Harmonies; it was the feeling they had of the inner structure of Nature; that the soul of all her voices and utterances was perfect music. Poetry, therefore, we call musical thought. The poet is he who thinks in that manner. At bottom, it turns still on power of intellect; it is a man's sincerity and depth of vision that makes him a poet. See deep enough and you see musically; the heart of Nature being everywhere music, if you can only reach it.* [12]

(from *The Hero as Poet*)

In an earlier section of this book we concentrated on the development of Imagination and inner picturing. Here it is more Inspiration that concerns us, an inner listening for the right next word – both its sound and its meaning. Often in writing we can sense a rhyme or a resonance approaching long before it arrives, as though we were working within a field of musics and meanings where the whole is present in every part. It is possible to exercise this faculty.

Alliteration – the sounding together of consonants

Exercise 172
You can alliterate on each other's names: e.g.

> *Hesitating humble herbtea hero Herbert.*

Exercise 173
Give someone a letter of the alphabet, e.g. W, and then orally and spontaneously play with alliteration, using an introductory phrase:

> *I went into the garden and there I found .....*

> *a wish on the wind*
> *but it wouldn't woo me.*

Keep going with other letters until it flows.

Exercise 174

Also orally, you can make a spontaneous alliterative poem or story around the group, first word (or line) A, second word (or line) B, and so on.

Now, in writing, create an alliterative (perhaps nonsensical) verse. Many examples can be found in the Nursery Rhyme book: e.g.

> *Grey Goose and Gander*
> *Waft your wings together*
> *Carry the good King's daughter*
> *Over the one-strand river.*

Rhyme

Already, in other contexts, simple rhyming forms have been suggested. Now we can take it up as a conscious practice, as a training of the ear:

Exercise 175

Orally, rhyme around the group:

> *cat mat fat hat etc*
> *mother smother other brother etc.*

then alternately:

> *think bird drink heard ink third etc.*

and then repeat it several times with the same words.

Exercise 176

Now everyone write two rhyming words, and read them around:

> *think drink bird heard mat cat etc*

You can find other ways. These can be good kindling exercises before more serious writing.

Exercise 177

Compose a limerick (about people in the group):

Across the Channel, Monique
Came wanting to learn how to speak.
She returned to Paris
And said 'Listen to me',
But all that came out was a squeak.

Exercise 178
Compose a clerihew: e.g.

> *What I like about Clive*
> *Is that he is no longer alive.*
> *There is a great deal to be said*
> *For being dead.*[13]

(E. Clerihew Bentley)

[for more complicated rhyming forms see *p. 159*]

Tongue Twisters

Exercise 179
After practising some of the well-known tongue twisters: e.g.

> *Peggy Babcock. (10 times)*
>
> *Unique New York.*
>
> *Coffee from a proper copper coffee-pot.*

you can compose some of your own: e.g.

> *Six figs for the wicked wig-fixer.*
>
> *Five or six fickle sicklers scythed and sighed.*
>
> *Give gloves and a sieve to Sid's lovely sister.*
>
> *Whose hose do you suppose Hugh's used?*
> *His I suppose whose hose Hugh chose.*
> *And who do you suppose has used Hugh's hose?*
> *He who supposed Hugh's hose was his.*

N.B. Good tongue twisters have a better chance of immortality than bad epics.

Tongue Assisters

Exercise 180
Orally, pass a word around, slightly altering it each time – e.g.

> *Bible, rifle, ripple, triple, trickle,*
> *treacle, equal, eagle ...*

Exercise 181
Write some sentences in which there is a progression from word to word in a recognizable pattern of sounds. Don't think too hard about it – the meanings are not too important to begin with: e.g.

> *Neverthless last lammas a famous film*
> *limited the nostrils.*
>
> *Flumox a potential uncle cufflink*
> *locked in a hollyhock.*
>
> *Absolute lutenists insist on a zany tune,*
> *moonbread and mothcream between mouthfuls.*

We are still working here with rhyme and alliteration, but they are more deeply hidden within the words.

A master of this was Gerard Manley Hopkins. Here is a fine example in which the meanings are also important:

> *– is there any any, is there none such, nowhere known some bow or*
> *brooch or braid or brace, lace, latch or catch or key to keep back*
> *beauty, keep it, beauty, beauty, beauty from vanishing away?*[14]
> (from *The Leaden Echo and the Golden Echo*)

Exercise 182
Write an echo poem, either as a conversation or as a single voice: e.g.

> *As I stand here by the window*
> > *a widow*
> *I gaze out over the bare field*
> > *thrilled*
> *by a sudden birdsong*
> > *burdened*
> *by nothing now.*
> > *Sing now.*
> (with Katie Pettit)

Ask a partner to be your echo.

Exercise 183
Take one word as a seed of a piece of writing, and let it grow organically
from there. Concentrate mainly on the sound progressions, but let
meanings arise if they want to. Try, at least, to keep some unity of
mood. Obey the necessities of rhythm and resonance. [see also *exercise
248*]. e.g. (with fairly self-contained lines):

> cormorant
> corn in movement
> more corn moves
> cause a morning chorus
> crows caw raucously
> they cawed then rose of course
> cawing and cautiously crossing
> more and more, tossing lost
> cussing the raw air
> caw raw, caw raw
> daring to discuss
> in mournful chorus.

Or more freely, flowing from one line to the next: e.g.

> Rhododendrum.
> Roll the dough in a drum
> Drum the roll into dough.
> How do you roll through dough
> in a den without a dough roll?
> Drinking rum we beat our drums
> drumming doden roden dendo dum
> hordo rum mud eden doad.
> The road home was through the dreary den
> of rain soaked drums and dried up men.
> Hey ro, give me some dough
> so I can do what you do.
> And the drum beats on, the
> Rhododendrum doddles and
> murmurs on down the road.
>   (Daniel Stokes)

Exercise 184
Take a noun and, making it the first word of a sentence, find the other
words out of the remaining letters: e.g.

GRASS Raises A Slender Salad.
MAGIC Allows Giants Into Classrooms.
STAR Trembles and Remembers.
CREATION Risks Everything At The Insistence Of Nothing.
CREATION Roars Enormous Alphabets That Inwardly Order Nothingness.
CREATION Rolls Eggs And Terrors Into Owls Nests.
CREATION Rolls Every Act Towards Its Own Nemesis.
CREATION Rests Energetic At The Inside Of Nouns.
CREATION Rises Expressively And Triumphs In our Names.
CREATION Receives Eventually All Things Into One Name.

You can do the same with each other's names: e.g.

> *CATHERINE Admits The Heart's Eternal Royalty Is Never Easy.*

Gilgamesh, you may remember, [*p. 63*] wanted to leave his name stamped on brick. We have spent 5000 years doing that, though, and can surely trust our names now to the water:

Exercise 185
Write your name backwards and then speak it: e.g.

HSEMAGLIG

Exercise 186
Rearrange the letters of your name (or someone else's) so that it reveals who you really are: e.g.

PAUL MATTHEWS becomes MEAT PLUS WHAT.

It is always possible to find nasty things. Try, however, to find their Fabulous Name, some image to live by.

Exercise 187
Find all the words concealed in someone's name and then use them in a poem – the poem of their name.

Exercise 188
Write an acrostic, i.e. each line beginning with a letter of a person's name.

   If nothing else, these are all good exercises for helping group-awareness. [see also *exercise 86*]

Naming (2)

Having indulged for a while in language mainly for the sound's sake, we can turn now to consider more closely the relationship between sound and meaning. Previously [*p. 38*] we looked at naming as an act of definition. Perhaps there is more to it than that.

If we imagine further into the biblical story of Adam naming the animals [*p. 22*], we can ask – did he label each beast with an arbitrary noise, saying 'let us agree that this noise stands for that animal'? That is rather crudely put, but basically it is the modern view:

> *In the first place, any language is arbitrary. This means that there is nothing – or at most very little – in the nature of the things we talk about that dictates or controls the language we use to talk about them. When we are children we do not know this. We believe that the connection between an act or an object and the word which refers to it is somehow a natural and inevitable one. If you ask a child why he calls a certain object a 'clock', he will probably answer, "Because it is a clock." We can see the error of this belief in this childlike form. But it is likely to persist in a somewhat more sophisticated form in the minds of those who have not thought or studied about language. All of us have heard people make statements like "The real name for these things is 'crullers,' but I call them 'doughnuts' because everybody else around here does." Note the assumption that there is a real – natural or inevitable – name for something, even though nobody uses it. Only when we learn a foreign language do we become completely disabused of this notion. When we discover that 'horloge' and 'Uhr' seem to other people just as natural names for a timepiece as 'clock', we come to realise that none of them is really natural, but all are arbitrary.*[15]

(W. Nelson Francis)

This is taken from the introduction to a book about the English Language. On the one hand it can be accepted as a statement honest to the materialistic assumptions of our culture; on the other hand you might feel it embodies the slightly arrogant tone of the modern academic who thinks he has all the answers.

The 'childlike error' that Francis refers to is beautifully illustrated in the following extract from Piaget's *The Child's Conception of Life*. One of his helpers is questioning a 7 year old boy:

> *Where is the name of the Sun? Inside.*
> *What? Inside the sun...*
> *Where is the name of the clouds? Inside them too.*
> *Where is your name?.... I was given it.*
> *Yes, but where is your name? It's written down.*
> *Where? In the book.....*
> *How is the name of the Sun inside the sun?*
> *What do you mean? Because it's hot.*
> *If we could open the sun, should we see its name? No.*
> *And why is the name of the clouds inside the clouds?*
> *Because they are grey.*
> *And where is the name of the lake? On it.*
> *Why? Because it is not in it.*
> *Why not? Because there's water there.*
> *Why is the name on the lake? Because it*
> *can't go in, it doesn't go into it.*
> *But is the word "lake" on it? What does that mean?*
> *Is it written? No.*
> *Why is it on it? Because it can't go into it.*
> *Is it on top of it then? No.*
> *Where is it? It isn't anywhere.* [16]

This is rather a sad interview, really. It is clear that the interviewer thinks that he knows the true answer, and he ends the conversation when he succeeds in imposing this upon the child.

In William Blake's painting on the front cover of this book we have quite a different view. There is Adam under the Oak, his left hand on the serpent's head, the serpent's head upon his breast. Adam's eyes gaze both inwards and outwards at the same time, and he raises his right hand, one finger pointing upwards. His whole body is listening, waiting for the name as the animals move through his larynx.

Another poet, Ralph Waldo Emerson, has this to say about the act of naming:

> *The poet is the namer or language maker, naming things sometimes after their appearance, sometimes after their essence, and giving to every one its right name and not another's .... thereby rejoicing the intellect, which delights in detachments or boundary .... The poet names the thing because he sees it, or*

comes one step closer to it than any other. This expression or
naming is not art, but a second nature, grown out of the first, as
a leaf on a tree. [17]

(from *The Poet*)

Sound Sense

Between Mr. Francis and Mr. Blake, then, there stands an important
question:

> *Do things have names because we can speak?*
> *Or, do we speak because things have names?*

– that is to say, is there any real correspondence between name and
thing, or is it indeed entirely arbitrary?

Facing this question we can again experience that strong conflict
between heart and head that we encountered earlier – between
'primitive' and modern, child and adult, philosopher and poet. It is
out of this conflict that poetry arises.

The magical view of language put forward by Blake and Emerson is
impossible to prove, of course. It is even difficult, in the face of modern
linguistic attitudes, to make a case for it; and yet for someone sensitive
to poetry it is also impossible to agree that poetry is merely 'what oft
was thought, but ne'er so well expressed'. The experience of poetry is
that it is indeed magical. To explore this further, however, means
finding a way to overcome the limitations both of our subjective
feelings and of our habitual ways of thinking. Even if we do not dismiss
the possibility that sound has sense, we hesitate to investigate further –
and wisely, perhaps, for *weak-minded people* (according to Arthur
Rimbaud) *beginning by thinking about the first letter of the alphabet would
soon rush into madness.* [18]

To test this threshold needs some courage, for sure, as witnessed by
Robert Duncan:

> *As I come needing wonder as the new shoots need water*
> *to the letter A*
> *that sounds its mystery in wave and in wane*
> *trembling I bent as if there were a weight in words*
> *like that old man bends under his age towards death.* [19]

(from *The Natural Doctrine*)

Some kind of death is involved. To 'know the bamboo', [*p. 24*] we have to sacrifice the subjective feelings through which we habitually view the world; and, similarly, to approach the essence of a sound we would need to die into its presence and attend to the subtle feelings that arise in us in response to it.

Steiner claimed that it was out of such a trained perception that he developed the art of Eurythmy, in which the gestures of sounds are made visible in movement. In relation to this he gives indications about the qualities of each consonant. It would be hopelessly abstract, however, to catalogue them briefly here. Better would be to engage you in your own exploration.

Exercise 189

Compose an alphabet piece in which you attempt to enter truly into the qualities of each vowel and consonant. One poet who attempted this was Christopher Smart (but he was mad already). In his *Jubilate Agno* he has several alphabet lists: e.g.

> *For A is the beginning of learning*
> *and the door of heaven.*
> *For B is a creature busy and bustling.*
> *For C is a sense quick and penetrating.*
> *For D is depth.*
> *For E is eternity – such is the power*
> *of English letters taken singly ....*[20]

You can probably improve on this.

Vowels

Not so difficult to entertain is the idea that there is a connection between the quality of the different vowel sounds and our various emotions. We know this from the cries that arise (spontaneously?) in our immediate response to the world:

Ah!   – the cry of wonder that Plato says must precede all true philosophy.

Ooo!   – (as in 'moon') has something of mystery in it, and fear.

Oh!   – Sympathy, surprise

E!   – (as in 'me') pain, self-awareness.

The vowels have been ascribed by Rudolf Steiner to the different planets:[21]

Ao	I	A	E	O	A	OO
(now) –	(my) –	(say) –	(be) –	(for) –	(far) –	(Soon)
Sun	Moon	Mars	Mercury	Jupiter	Venus	Saturn

This has no immediate use for the writer, but to work with it in imagination can help redeem our words from the poverty they have fallen into in modern times.

Exercise 190
Speak some of your previous pieces, leaving out all the consonants.

Exercise 191
Compose some pieces which bring out the quality of particular vowels.

Consonants

Rudolf Steiner also makes a connection between the consonants and the zodiac, seeing them as creative archetypes which formed us and which can continue to work formatively and healingly in our speaking:[22]

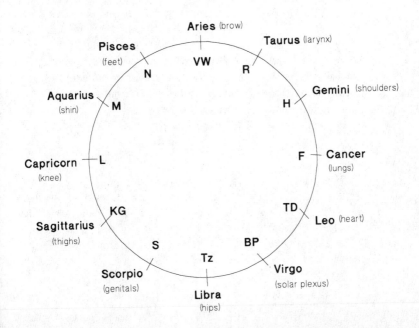

Consonants, unlike the vowels, are shapers, defining the outer world. They are usually grouped according to their place in the mouth when spoken:

> Labial – BPMW; Dental – FVSShCZ;
> Lingual – NDTL; Palatal – GKChNg

Steiner also groups them in relation to the four elements:[23]

Fire: H Ch Y Sh S Th F W V Z

Air: R

Water: L

Earth: D T B P G K M N

In Medieval times people looked back to the fall of the tower of Babel, as the moment when things fell away from their true names:

> *And the whole earth was of one language, and of one speech. And it came to pass, as they journeyed from the east, that they found a plain in the land of Shinar; and they dwelt there. And they said one to another, Go to, let us make brick, and burn them thoroughly. And they had brick for stone, and slime had they for mortar. And they said, Go to, let us build a city and a tower, whose top may reach unto heaven; and let us make a name, lest we be scattered abroad upon the face of the whole earth. And the Lord came down to see the city and the tower, which the children of men builded. And the Lord said, behold, the people is one, and they have all one language; and this they begin to do; and now nothing will be restrained from them, which they have imagined to do. Go to, let us go down, and there confound their language, that they might not understand one another's speech. So the Lord scattered them abroad from thence upon the face of all the earth: and they left off to build the city. Therefore the name of it is called Babel.*[24]
>
> (*Genesis*, Ch.11)

Yet maybe we are not utterly 'confounded':

Coleridge in his preface to *Kubla Khan* [*p. 38*] describes how in his dream *all images rose up .... as things, with a parallel production of their correspondent expressions.* Elsewhere he speaks of a *light in sound, a sound-like power in light* [25] – i.e. a link between name and thing. We can test this:

Fictionary

Exercise 192
Everyone make up a new noun. Choose two of them –

e.g. *Withwothel* and *Zagaratad*

Is one darker than the other? What size are they? Male or female? If they were food or drink which one would you prefer? If you had to meet one on a dark road which would you choose? Which one would you prefer to marry?

Exercise 193
Take a made-up word and ask everyone to write a definition of it. See if there is agreement. Do the same with a whole sentence.

Exercise 194
Find some words in the dictionary that are unknown to anyone in the group and pass them around on separate sheets of paper, asking each person to write a short dictionary style definition of its possible meaning – e.g.

> *Shagreen – a wild vegetable used in salads.*
> *– a mythical being found in woods and forests*
> *– an agreement between gentlemen.*

Or it can be done without seeing what other people wrote. Ask one member of the group to read out all the definitions of one of the words, including the correct answer (slightly altered to sound less formal), and then try to guess which is the right definition and then who wrote which definition.

This is a fun game, and at the same time it is a test of the statement that 'words do not have meaning for people, people have meanings for words'. Don't just invent meanings. Listen for what the sounds want to mean. If God had said, 'Let there be WHIMBREL', what would have appeared? Also write a sentence in which the word is used correctly, according to your definition:

Whimbrel:

– *An instrument the wind plays on: 'The whimbrel was ringing in the wind.'*
– *Nautical Knot employed for temporary use: 'Put a whimbrel there, but stay by it.'*

– One afraid to admit wrong-doing: 'Everyone heard the quiver in that whimbrel's lying voice.'
– A small bird that flies across the sea crying 'whim, whim': 'How lonely the cry of the whimbrel sounds tonight.'

Translation

Earlier [*p. 119*] a modern denial of the magical connection between name and thing was quoted:

When we discover that 'Horloge' and 'Uhr' seem to other people just as natural a name for a timepiece as 'clock', we come to realize that none of them is natural, but all are arbitrary.

But is this really so?

Arbre   Tree   Baum

Exercise 195
Draw underneath each of these names the kind of tree that the word conjures up for you: its size, its gesture. Is there agreement in the group? Or don't even draw it – let your body assume the appropriate gesture. Do the same with

Flower	*Fleur*	*Blume*	(including colours)
Head	*Tête*	*Kopf*	*Cabeza*
I	*Je*	*Ich*	*Jo*

Different nations, it seems, experience trees differently, hence the difference in name – they are naming, exclaiming, their relationship to the thing, as well as defining an aspect of the thing itself.

Exercise 196
Take a short passage in a language you do not understand and translate it into English as best you can. If done in the group give a general indication of the mood beforehand.

Exercise 197
If there are, for instance, two German speakers in the group, have two groups working on a translation of the same short poem – giving the correct meaning, but also trying to make a beautiful English poem out of it. Compare translations.

Exercise 198

It is a good test for poetry to compare different translations of the same piece. Your ear will at once tell you which one is best; then you can look more closely and see why: e.g.

Three lines from Rilke's poem 'Autumn Day':[26]

a) Lord, it is time. The Summer was too long.
Lay now thy shadow over the sundials,
And on the meadows let the wind blow strong.

b) Lord, it is time. The summer was so great.
Impose upon the sundials now your shadows
And round the meadows let the winds rotate.

c) Lord, it is time. The summer was so good.
Now lay your shadows on the sundial's face
And let the winds run loose on field and wood.

d) Lord, it is time. The summer was most great.
Lay your shadow on the sundials
And on the fields let the winds loose.

Here is the original:

e) Herr: es ist Zeit. Der Sommer war sehr groß
Leg deinen Schatten auf die Sonnenuhren
Und auf den Fluren laß die Winde los.

Make an even better version.

The English language (as we have seen before, *p.* 39) is actually a compound of two languages – Anglo-Saxon and Latin (through the French), and it is still possible to translate from one to the other, as can be seen from a comparison of the following passages:

> *As we walked up the hill, we saw that the path had been set every few yards with a heap of stones. This we understood was to help wayfarers, whose road took them across the moors in winter, when the snow lay deep and hid the way. But when we reached the top, there were no more stones, or if there were, the heather had overgrown them and they could not be seen. The path petered out and we had to make our way as best we could through the heather, keeping always to the top of the ridge.*

> *As we ascended the incline, we noticed that the track had been marked at intervals with piles of rocks. This we recognised was to aid travellers whose route traversed the mountains in winter, when the snow lay deep and concealed the line of the track. But*

*when we finally attained the summit, the rocks were no longer
visible; either they were covered by herbage or were non-
existent. The track gradually disappeared and we were forced
to choose a route through the heather, taking as a guide to our
direction the crest of the incline.*

The first passage uses predominantly Saxon words, the second is more
Latinate. Read them carefully, exploring their different qualities.
Which one to do you prefer?

Exercise 199
List some of the synonyms: e.g.

hid	–	*concealed*
way	–	*direction*
saw	–	*noticed*
reached	–	*attained*
top	–	*summit*

But is there such a thing as a synonym? Besides the differentiations
that have occurred through use and association, does not every sound
insist upon a different shade of meaning?

Exercise 200
Look back on one of your previous pieces and try to discern which
words are Latin and which Saxon.

Exercise 201
Write a few sentences of your own using words that you feel are
derived from the Anglo-Saxon, and then translate them into a more
Latin form.

Exercise 202
Ask everyone in the group to translate the same sentence from Saxon to
Latin: e.g. (from *The Jumblies*, by Edward Lear)

*Far and few, far and few
Are the lands where the Jumblies live.*[27]

becomes

*Distant and infrequent, distant and infrequent,
are the territories which the Jumblies inhabit.*

Taken to such an extreme it can sound absurd, especially if the line translated is from a poem, where (presumably) the poet tried to find exactly the right word to carry both information and feeling. In the present example the 'Ah' and the 'Ooo' of the first three words carry a feeling which is completely lost in the reworking.

In moderation, however, a Latinate word can bring a refinement that is not possible with the Saxon. Shakespeare was a master of this: e.g.

> *Shall I* compare *thee to a Summer's day?*
> *Thou art more lovely and more* temperate.[28]

Characterization (2)

This exploration of the qualities of sounds brings us round once again to the work with definition or characterization that we began in section 2 of this book. We can pick up where we left off on page 54 where 'Language as music,' was referred to. In characterizing something we can try to find the qualities of sound and rhythm (as well as meaning) which belongs to it. As a first approach we will take subjects where there is an obvious link between quality of thing and quality of language.

Exercise 203
Compose a piece which embodies a particular mood or emotion – e.g. joy, inwardness, sorrow. Find the tone (and movement) which belongs to them. Already we have tried this with made up languages [*exercise 161*] and with nonsense language [*exercise 170*]. We can use what we learned there and bring it into meaningful composition. One way to do this is through conversation between opposites – e.g. happiness and sadness [see *exercise 127*] in which you find the quality of voice best suited to the part chosen.

Exercise 204
Try the same with colours – either a conversation between two colours, or a piece in which a colour comes to expression through appropriate sounds and rhythms as well as through images.

This seems possible with colours because colours themselves hover between being outer thing and inner mood [see *exercise 62*].

The French poet Arthur Rimbaud, who tried to break through the limitations of consciousness by breaking the limits of language, speaks of his attempt:

I invented the colour of the vowels! A Black, E white, I red, O blue, U green – I made rules for the form and movement of each consonant, and with instinctive rhythms I flattered myself that I had created a poetic language accessible, some day, to all of the senses. I reserved translation rights. I expressed the inexpressible. I defined vertigoes.[29]

(from *A Season in Hell*)

In his sonnet, 'Voyelles' he also expresses the images that rise up for him in the presence of the vowels – e.g.

O – *sublime trumpet full of strange sounds, silences crossed by angels and by worlds!*[30]

If vowels have colours, then colours have vowels through which we can express them.

Exercise 205
Characterize once again the elements of fire, water, air, earth [see *exercise 158*], but this time allow the meanings to flow back: e.g.

Fire – *It laps and licks and smacks its lips*
      devouring all in ire or bliss.

Exercise 206
Turn now to particulars – e.g. a diamond, a rose, a tiger – subjects drawn from the different kingdoms of nature. It is best to take natural objects at first, for they still partake of the more general elemental forces that created them. Out of that recognition we can find an appropriate language for them.

In an earlier section [*exercise 58*] we tried to characterize the differences between mineral, plant and animal, and as you work with them now note which aspects of language arise in response to them.

To the eye of the Imagination they themselves are a grammar and a language:

The minerals – nature's nouns – seem to require strong consonants.

The plants and flowers – the Earth's adjectives and vowels.

The animals – they are the verbs of nature, and seek expression in the rhythms of our language. [see *exercise 252*]

– it is an equation worth making, but it needs to be forgotten afterwards.

Finally, we can come right down to earth and speak of things made by humans – beautiful things, useful things, but also 'the guts and innards of the weeping coughing car', for instance, that Allen Ginsberg saw dumped on the riverside. Poets do not turn up their noses at such things (which, seemingly, have fallen away from the natural orders that sustain poetry) but, by naming them beautifully, gather them back into the context of meaning. Ginsberg's craft allows us to look through (not at) his language, into the significance of the scene which moved him.[31]

This is not to be confused with that popular but somewhat facile kind of verse in which sounds merely imitate the noise of the subject matter – e.g. John Masefield's:

> *Dirty British coaster with a salt-caked smoke stack,*
> *Butting through the Channel in the mad March days.*[32]

> (from 'Cargoes')

We admire the craft, but there is a need now to move beyond exercises (where the correspondence between sound and meaning is consciously worked at) towards a more spontaneous creating in which any 'value' that a sound might have takes on infinite shades in relation to the whole sound-field of the poem.

GOD'S GRANDEUR by Gerard Manley Hopkins.

> *The world is charged with the grandeur of God.*
> *It will flame out like shining from shook foil;*
> *It gathers to a greatness, like the ooze of oil*
> *Crushed. Why do men then now not reck his rod?*
> *Generations have trod, have trod, have trod;*
> *And all is seared with trade; bleared, smeared with toil;*
> *And wears man's smudge and shares man's smell; the soil*
> *Is bare now, nor can foot feel, being shod.*

> *And for all this, nature is never spent;*
> *There lives the dearest freshness deep down things;*
> *And though the last lights off the black West went*
> *Oh, morning, at the brown brink eastward, springs –*
> *Because the Holy Ghost over the bent*
> *World broods with warm breast and with ah! bright wings.*[33]

In the first stanza of this poem we can see the poet working with all the 'devices' of poetry that we have been exploring – rhyme, alliteration, assonance, onomatopoeia, the qualities of the elements – but here they are not devices. Through a long devotion to his craft Hopkins has formed himself into a fit instrument to receive the inspiration when it comes to him. In this poem the form and content of the language coincide, so that each becomes a revelation of the other, and when that happens we can hardly deny that we are in the presence of the magical. This is especially the case in the last verse, the last two lines, where (no longer imitating anything external) the progression of the vowels exactly accords with the movement of the heart as it opens in wonder and sings the Creation.

Five

The Command

COMMAND is language as deed, where the sentence is dynamic, imposing will on the world – not what language says, but what it does. Strength is the ideal it strives for, power for the good.

Before coming to writing we can approach it orally:

Exercise 207
Grant someone the power to organize an event in the room through the responsible exercise of command. Some courage is needed to take this on.

Exercise 208
Sit back to back with a partner, with a set of identical objects (blocks of various colours, shapes, sizes) on the tables in front of you. Arrange them one at a time while directing the other, through commands, to do likewise. The partner (with, or without questions) should follow, arranging the blocks according to instructions. Compare the results afterwards, the observers commenting upon how uncertainties arose.

Exercise 209
Remember, and share, some of the commands which dominated and shaped your childhood: e.g.

> *Brush your teeth. Don't speak until you are spoken to. Don't talk to strangers.*

Can you remember the 'Ten Commandments'?

Exercise 210
Approach the place where you are (or a painting [see *exercise 1*]) through command: e.g.

> *Make a bright flame, candle. Sing with all your might, you birds. Watch, keep your hands still to give us more time. Plants, breathe out as much oxygen as you possibly can. Trees, stand straight and tall. Light-bulbs, glow brightly but don't dazzle us. Table, stop moving around so much. Fire, blow your warmth over here. Chair, be a support for me. Blow away, clouds, so I can see the stars. Stay there, wall, and hold the ceiling up.*

(Nick Huber)

Which is more powerful: 'Fire, blow your warmth,' or, 'Blow your warmth, fire'?

The full power of the command, though you may not wish to use it, is to be found within the verbs – e.g. 'Go'. 'Stop.' – and the longer the command becomes the more it becomes something else.

In the example above it is not people who are commanded, but chairs and candles. We could take that further:

Exercise 211
Write commandments for inanimate things: e.g. One commandment for the clock –

> *Tick before tocking.*

Or for plants: e.g. Three commandments for the buttercup –

> *Shine yellow under a child's chin.*
> *Grow beautifully in the worst places.*
> *Grace the grasses.*

Or for animals: e.g. Eight commandments for the wild Tibetan donkey –

> *Accept neither pack nor saddle.*
> *Pay no heed to the stick.*
> *Run faster than your own wild shadow.*
> *Jump over seven mountains.*
> *Dance on the highest peak.*
> *Hullabaloo in the foothills.*
> *Disturb the monks at their prayers.*
> *Shake the equilibrium of their prayerwheels.*

You can imagine them as instructions given by the Creator, whether divine or human.

This can be done by passing a paper round the group, and each adding a few; or as a more sustained individual piece: e.g.

> *Stop raining*
> *Rain somewhere else*
> *Rain on those who deserve wetness*
> *Rain on Sally's new shoes*
> *Be proper rain*
> *Rain properly*
> *Rain upside down, sideways*
> *Rain in curves*
> *Rain too early to be heard*

> *Rain on the new sown grain*
> *Rain when I'm lonely.*

It might seem strange to give commands to things which cannot respond, yet the first verse of a well-known poem demonstrates the emotional power of it:

> *Go, lovely Rose –*
> *Tell her that wastes her time and me*
> *That now she knows,*
> *When I resemble her to thee,*
> *How sweet and fair she seems to be.*[1]
> (Edmund Waller)

Exercise 212
Write the commands that an object, a plant, an animal might speak to us: e.g.

> *Forget-me-not.*
> *Plant your feet carefully.*
> *Find your own eyes in the blue of me.*

It is not often that we find sustained use of command in literature. Cookery books, car manuals, instructions for ordering events and rituals, are some examples. This book is another.

Exercise 213
Write an invitation piece. It could begin with something similar to T.S. Eliot's –

> *Come in under the shadow of this red rock*
> *and I will show you ......*[2]

Exercise 214
Compose some small titled events: e.g.

> *KNIFE EVENT:*
> *Lay it close to your heart.*
>
> *TEETH EVENT:*
> *Laugh.*
>
> *SHADOW EVENT:*
> *Pretend you don't have one.*

LONELY EVENT:
Write yourself a letter.

DEATH EVENT:
Open wide the window by the sea.
Put on a flowing white dress.
Light two candles.
Lie down on a soft blue bed.
Lie comfortably.
Call in three black mourners, sighing.
Gaze wisely upon them.
Listen. Close eyes quietly.
Breathe out.
                    (Diane Proskauer)

Quite simple everyday events, like dressing or standing at bus-stops, take on added significance if directed in this way: e.g.

PHOTOGRAPH EVENT:
Adjust the swivelling seat.
Insert one pound. Comb the fringe.
Look happy. Natural.
And smile
   smile
   smile
   smile.

There are some well-known stage directions which take a metaphorical form; e.g. *Make hay while the sun shines.*

Exercise 215
Make up some new proverbs in the form of commands.

Magic

Tell everyone in the group to stand up, and when they have done so you can discuss whether that was an example of the magic power of the word. For that must be our next consideration – does the power of language lie only in its meanings being responded to, or do its forms and movements work some deeper magic?

Certainly children have a sense for such possibilities when they chant:

> *Snow snow faster*
> *Alley alley blaster.*
>   or
> *Rain rain go away*
> *Come again another day.*

– a sense which adults have lost, apart from their fear of certain 'obscene ' or 'unlucky' words. For children even the gibberish of counting-out rhymes' [*exercise 162*] has an underlying seriousness. To say a word can make you immune in a game of 'He'. Give your word in the playground, and there is hell to pay if you break it.

It is the so-called primitive's experience that names are part of the things, and for this reason people fear to reveal their names lest that knowledge be used against them. Children admit to such a fear when they feel it necessary to deny it by chanting:

> *Sticks and stones may break my bones*
> *But names will never hurt me.*

If you tell each other your middle names, or your nicknames, you can experience something of this vulnerability.

Concerning the language of very ancient peoples, Rudolf Steiner has this to say:

> ..... *The speech which they produced had something of the power of nature. They not only named things, but in their words was a power over things and also over their fellow men. ......*
> *When a Rmoahals man produced a word, it developed a power similar to that of the object designated. Because of this, words at that time were curative; they could advance the growth of plants, tame the rage of wild animals, and perform similar functions .... For them language was especially sacred. The misuse of a certain sound, which possessed an important power, was an impossibility. Each man felt that such misuse could cause him immense harm. The good magic of such words would have changed into its opposite. .... In a kind of innocence of feeling the Rmoahals ascribed their power not so much to themselves as to the divine nature acting through them.* [3]

It was Steiner's view that in the course of human evolution we have fallen from such a *will* language (some cultures more than others), through a *feeling* language, into a language of *intellect* where words are experienced as little more than labels for concepts. In other words, language that was all poetry in the beginning has gradually died into its prose content.

Without some sense of the magical power of language, poetry is clearly impossible. We may not be able to create light simply by naming it [see *p. 22*], but with our words we can act upon each other with immense potential for good or ill. A word has the power to change a person's level of consciousness:

Exercise 216
Make up a lullaby – an obvious example of language having power beyond its conceptual meaning: e.g.

> *Go to sleep, Pink-Bloom,*
> *The horse will not drink.*
> *Go to sleep, Rose-bush,*
> *The horse begins to cry.*[4]
> (from *Blood Wedding*, F.G. Lorca).

The sounds and rhythms must induce sleep in the child, who grasps not our meanings but our intention.

Exercise 217
Make up a mouth-watering menu, perhaps using a mixture of English and made-up language.

Exercise 218
Compose a grace to be said before a meal: e.g.

> *Before the flour the mill,*
> *Before the mill the grain,*
> *Before the grain the sun and the rain,*
> *The beauty of God's will.*

Graces are out of fashion, but their potential is to enhance our appreciation of the food so that it nourishes both soul and body. A grace well-spoken can transform bread-breaking into communion and com-pan-ionship (= 'with bread') [see *exercise 143* and *exercise 300*].

Exercise 219
Make a wish poem, this time emphasizing its command aspect: e.g.

> *Star light, star bright,*
> *First star I see tonight,*
> *I wish I may, I wish I might*
> *Have the wish I wish tonight.*

It becomes a magic spell, with the power woven into the very spelling and sounding of the words. This becomes obvious if we consider what is lost when we extract its prose content:

> *I wish by the first star I see tonight that I might have my wish.*

This conveys pretty much the same information, but the power goes slack.

The wish stands, curiously, between statement, exclamation, question and command, partaking of each of them.

Exercise 220
Make a charm: e.g.

> *May the Humming Bird lull our fears.*
> *May the Wren remember us.*
> *May the Raven never forget his books and his learning.*
> *May the Owl find an answer at last to her only question.*
> *May the Sparrow never lament that he is not an Eagle.*
> *May the Eagle never despise us.*
> *May the door be opened for the Woodpecker.*
> *May the Parrot persevere in his education.*
> *May the Lapwing give over grieving.*
> *May the Lark build her airy tower.*
> *May the Nightingale return at last to our branches.*

'May' is more a permission than a command. It is, nonetheless, a word of power:

Exercise 221
Make a love charm.

Exercise 222
Weave a spell to bless or protect: e.g.

> *May the circle of circles surround you*
> *And the point of all points be your star:*

> *May the light of lights as lantern*
> *Bring the love of your life from afar.*
>
> (Duncan Macintosh)

'Let' is another word of power. The strength of the following charm against witchcraft lies, again, partly in the repetition:

> *Let sky turn topsy-turvy*
> *Let earth be up-turned*
> *Let horns sprout on horse and ass*
> *Let whiskers grow on a girl's face*
> *Let dry cow-dung sink, stones swim*
> *But let this charm not falter.*[5]
>
> (reworking of trans. by Verrier Elwin)

But its use of paradox also contains a power. By taking the static, created world back to its origins where everything is still possible, a healing source is found (i.e. one that makes whole) and the evil is rendered powerless [see *exercise 300* and *p. 36*].

Fire

At the beginning of each section of this book we have looked at the ideals that are contained within the four kinds of sentence that we find in grammar. We should not be blind, however, to the fact that 'the tongue is a fire,' and that unless it is governed 'it defileth the whole body, and setteth on fire the course of nature' (The Epistle of James). Statement can serve the lie; command has the power to wound; exclamation can easily turn to slander; and when we approach people or the world without real questions then our language becomes trivial.

For this fire to serve the good we need to foster a connection with helpful sources.

Exercise 223
Compose an invocation – for personal use, or to be used at a poetry reading: [e.g. see *p. x*]

Exercise 224
Or write a letter to your muse, asking for inspiration.

Epic poets, of course, are famous for their invocations. 'Sing, Oh Muse', begins Homer. 'Hail, Holy Light,' exclaims Milton, 'How shall I express thee unblamed?' – placing themselves in a context larger than their personal skills and opinions, letting their own voice become an instrument for some higher source, for that which has to be spoken.

Some form of 'kindling' as the Arab poets called it, needs to be present at the beginning of each group session – small exercises to awaken the mind's eye and ear and sense of movement.

Movement

Command is not really language as information; rather, it is that which is in formation; it is craft ('Kraft' = power); it is a movement through the sentence which can take many forms and gestures:

> *SOMETHING IS MOVING*
> *I let it move through me.*
> *I let it move by means of me.*
> *I let it move by my means.*
> *I let it move towards what it means.*
> *It means to me through me.*
> *It means to move through me*
> *As it is meant for me, I mean.*
> *I let it until it is through with me.*[6]
>   (Robert Duncan).

Language as will [see *p. 139*] comes to expression in how the language moves. Statement, Question, Exclamation, Command are acts of language that we can practise wordlessly.

Exercise 225
We can draw them:

Statement: ☐ or ● or ____, a 'complete thought,' with boundaries towards the universe.

Question: We have the question-mark already – ? – arising, surely, out of a sense for sentence as gesture. Like an ear, was suggested earlier, but taken back into movement it becomes a spiralling maybe.

Exclamation: We have the exclamation mark – ! – but we might see it also as a fountain.

Command: → a pointing.

Exercise 226
We can do the same with hand gestures.

Exercise 227
Or with the whole body, engaging in some of the basic athletic activities:

Grammar and Gymnastics

Throughout this book language as movement has been emphasized, and many exercises in throwing, wrestling, stamping, clapping, etc. have been suggested as ways to prepare for the act of writing. Long ago, Aristotle recognized in his Peripatetic (i.e. 'walking') school of philosophy the relation between moving and thinking; and the connection between motor function and language is fully acknowledged in modern speech and writing therapy. If someone lacks the inner form to write or to speak a clear sentence they would do well to work with gymnastics, which can at times be sheer grammar, sentences without information attached. Through articulating the joints of our bodies we can learn to articulate our words clearly.

It comes very naturally to us to speak of a true person as one who stands by their word. Many expressions for morality, in fact, are taken from bodily posture or spatial direction – right = straight, wrong = wrung, crook, sinister, bent, on the level, twisted, spineless, upright, high, low, back-handed, are just some of them. A genuine gymnastics would be concerned with cultivating truth, beauty and strength in the moral life as well as outer physical prowess. These were certainly the ideals behind the pentathlon event of the ancient Olympic games – running, jumping, wrestling, discus-throwing, spear-throwing. They embody a grammar of action which can be taken up into language and thinking. Some exercises, of course, require specialist gymnastic teachers, but many described in the various sections of this book can, with practice, be worked with by anyone.

Exercise 228
The Command, itself, finds expression in spear-throwing or, more simply, in throwing a ball or beanbag (overarm) to a partner, or at a target. Direct flight towards an aim is its proper signature.

Exercise 229
Come back to words now and write your own signature in the air,

everyone in turn. Observe it as a dance, as gesture, how it reveals and betrays your various energies.

Exercise 230
Write your signature on the paper. Graphologists would have us believe that it signifies not just the sound of its characters, but the very character of the writer.

Turn it upside down: e.g. William Shakespeare's signature:

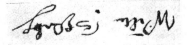

and consider what inward movement it is the trace of. You can do the same with doodles. In Blake's illuminated books the handwriting dissolves sometimes into sheer squiggle and energy before returning to its conventional channels; and in numerous Renaissance paintings of the 'Annunciation' the words that issue from the Angel's lips towards Mary take the form of a spiralling scroll: e.g.

Lukas Van Leyden: 'Annunciation' (detail)

This Word does more than tell – it impregnates.

Exercise 231
Can you decipher this disc that was found at Phaestos in Crete (no one else can)?:

The fact that some cultures write from left to right while others write right to left or from top to bottom, or even (as here) in a spiral, is perhaps also the signature of an inner movement.

What is a Sentence?

Dictionary-makers favour the idea that a sentence is a 'complete thought' – whatever that may be.

Exercise 232
Write a short sentence word for word backwards, then read it forwards: e.g.

> *Sentence short a is this.*

This does not accord with the definition, yet it is possible to read it in such a way that it sounds complete.

Exercise 233
Now write it letter for letter backwards: e.g.

> *Ecnetnes trohs a si siht.*

Exercise 234
Or (yet again), write a sentence in a new language – not as expression of feeling this time [see *exercise 158*], but as sheer energy in formation.

These, too, though they lack thought content, can satisfy our sense for sentences.

As you listen to each other's sentences try to be aware of how each one, in its different way, engages your breathing. The movement of our breath in and out is, in fact, our human sentence, and is the deeper measure of whether something is a sentence or not.

Ernest Fenollosa: *The sentence form was forced upon primitive men by nature itself. It is not we who made it; it was a reflection of the temporal order in causation. All truth can be expressed in sentences because all truth is a transference of power. The type of sentence in nature is a flash of lightning.*[7]

Exercise 235
Write one long sentence together in the group, passing a paper round and each adding a word in turn [see *exercise 116*].

Exercise 236
Write, individually now, a long sentence: e.g.

> *The prison across the street is undoubtedly full of murderers and arsonists but even they this morning are simply brushing their teeth or opening letters from their mothers.*

Listen to how it moves – straight, or in curves. Does it lose energy before the end? Are there any superfluous words or bad constructions which block or dissipate that energy? Compare the shape of your sentence with someone else's: e.g.

> *Betsy ran five miles uphill trying to catch her dog who was in heat and had managed to escape from the house when the door was opened briefly to take in the milk and was getting farther and farther away from her as the climb was steep and slow for so fat a person.*

(Phoebe Wedin)

Notice how important little words like 'and' and 'but' are in directing the energy.

Exercise 237
Give your sentence to someone else to improve. Try the constructions other ways, but keep the same words and information. Try to fit the form as closely as possible to the content.

Exercise 238
Try the same thing, but using different words.

This balancing of the movements within the sentence can become so heightened that the need for the poetic line arises: e.g.

> *I found a face*
> *in the depths*
> *of day*
> *surrounded*
> *by the light*
> *that love*
> *lavishes*
> *upon all who*
> *serve her.*
> (Jaya Graves, Philippa Williams-Brett)

Exercise 239
Write such a one sentence poem, alternate lines with a partner ("no more than five words in a line"). If a true energy is moving through the poem then the right place to end will declare itself. Afterwards you can re-work the same words, trying different linebreaks. e.g.

> *I found a face*
> *in the depths of day*
> *surrounded by the light*
> *that love*
> *lavishes upon all*
> *who serve her.*

Read the various versions aloud, and consider which you prefer, and why. [for further work with 'free-verse', see *p. 172*].

Try some sentences in which the movement is determined by some of those small words which (though we hardly notice them) stitch the universe together – since, because, until, unless, although, if, but etc.

Exercise 240
This can be done collaboratively at first, using a known formula, but folding the paper before handing the sentence on to be completed: e.g.

> *I used to (be) ......*
> *but now ......*

or   *I seem to be .....*
> *but really .....*

or   *If you .....*
> *I .....*

or   *If I were .....*
> *I would .....*
> *and ....*
> *until .....*

or (taking the much imitated lines of the Chinese poet, Hsu-Kan):

> *Since you, Sir, went away*
> *my bright mirror*
> *is dim and untended.*[8]

Exercise 241
Lead this into individual compositions, exploring the energy contained in these words which we all understand and yet cannot explain to anyone. [e.g. *p. 152*].

Exercise 242
Compose, with a partner, some small poems in which the number of lines is pre-determined. One way to do this is by asking each partner to give 3(4, 5?) words to the other, and then to write a 6(8, 10?) line poem together, incorporating in turn one of the words in each line [see *exercise 119* for a conversational example].

Exercise 243
Compose, alternate lines with a partner, some diamond-shaped poems, the number of lines and words being pre-determined, and the number of words in a line expanding and contracting: e.g. (with three lines):

And	*What*
even you	*a nice*
smile.	*dungeon.*

(with five lines):

I	My	Along
like to	dry handkerchief	such muddy
pick up stones	is flying in	roads the poet
polished by	the unnoticed	slithers, and
others.	sadness.	sings.

(with seven lines):

Only	Hello
a tiny	little sparrow.
noise can frighten	Fly to me
you as you are.	when the north wind
Even a star	chills your wings.
falling hurts	I also
you.	sing.

They can also be made orally and spontaneously, with people stepping into the form as it is being created.

Exercise 244
Write a whole one yourself, and have a partner write a second, starting with your last word.

A good accompaniment to such an exercise is spear-throwing, for in language, too, the movement must not 'fall flat' or have any superfluous flourishes. It must carry through to the last word and 'stick in' with its tail pointing back to where it came from. That final word needs to arise out of the necessities set up by the previous movements, meanings, resonances, and yet bring a touch of surprise. Try to give meaning to the line breaks rather than creating chopped-up prose.

Exercise 245
Now (possibly with a partner) compose a haiku [see *p. 24*] in which the number of lines and syllables is pre-determined: e.g.

Little grasshopper	(5 syllables)
shelter from the midnight frost	(7 syllables)
in the scarecrow's sleeve.[9]	(5 syllables)

(Pablo Neruda, trans. Christopher Logue)

Previously this classical Japanese form was suggested as a means of intensifying the use of image. Consider it now as an intense field of energy where if one syllable is lax then the whole piece is ruined. It is most important how such poems are read aloud. Use the silence, compose it, as though it were a pond into which the pebble of the poem is dropped. Basho's poem about the frog [*p. 25*] exactly embodies the experience of listening to such poetry.

Exercise 246

Ask a partner to respond with another haiku, until a whole chain (or 'renga') is created.

Exercise 247

Take one haiku (or diamond-shaped poem) written in the group, and try to perfect it. Change lines around. Are the words all necessary? It would be true to say that it is easy to write bad haiku, difficult to write good ones (especially in English), but it would be even truer to say that good ones come in a flash, while the bad ones take endless labour.

Gradually, through these pages, we have been introducing more and more restrictions upon the movement of the sentences. In doing so, however, we acquire other freedoms. Why else would poets take on the elaborate forms that we are about to explore?

Verse

'Verse' as mentioned before, means a 'turning', the uni-verse being the 'one turning,' the poem that moves us all.

S.T. Coleridge: The common end of all narrative, nay of all poems, is to convert a series into a whole, to make these events, which in real or imagined History move on in a straight line, assume to our understandings a circular motion – the snake with its tail in its mouth.[10]

The maker of the Phaistos Disc [*p.145*] would understand that.

Exercise 248

Take a sentence and (at first with a partner) ring the changes on it: e.g.

I stood by the mountain edge.
The mountain stood by.
I edged by the mountain
feeling edgy to mount.
I stood by the edge stood I.
The mountain understood.
I stood under the mountain
and the mountain stood by.
I edged to the edge and stood.

(Adrian Locher, Phillippa Williams Brett)

It works best if you choose words which are happy to change their parts of speech. They should also have a strong pictorial and musical quality.

Poets can easily become so obsessed with this turning of the words that the play is everything. At its deepest level, however, it is the attempt to reach back into the primal Word that St. John speaks of:

In the beginning was the Word, and the Word was with God, and the Word was God. The same was in the beginning with God. All things were made by him, and without him was not anything made that was made. [11]

(*St. John*, Ch.1)

T.S. Eliot, in 'Ash Wednesday', also revolved around it:

If the lost word is lost, if the spent word is spent,
If the unheard, unspoken
Word is unspoken, unheard:
Still is the unspoken word, the Word unheard,
The Word without a word, the Word within
The world and for the world;
And the light shone in darkness and
Against the Word the unstilled world still whirled
About the centre of the silent Word. [12]

The most obvious and most ancient form of the turning poem is the use of repetition at the beginning of each line or paragraph. You will find many examples throughout this book – 'I am ..... I saw ..... I remember', and others. To be given such an anchor can, paradox-ically, be a freeing experience. [see also *p. 142*].

Exercise 249

Try using a repeated word or phrase as a binding device: e.g.

> *NANT-ADAM – a blessing*
>
> *If I knew a house to rest in*
> *it would be beside Adam's stream.*
> *and in the morning the warmth of sun on slates*
> *would wake me.*
>
> *If I knew a house to rest in*
> *it would have a garden with a bench just*
> *outside the backdoor*
> *where I would sit in the sun and sip tea*
>
> *If I knew a house to rest in*
> *it would have a field beyond the garden*
> *and beyond the field a wood with a stream*
> *to run thru*
>
> *If I knew a house to rest in*
> *there would be clouds as high as the sky*
> *and a buzzard circling round*
> *with his wings outstretched and all his*
> *fingers pointing*
>
> *If I knew a house to rest in*
> *we would (just before sleep came)*
> *stand beneath the stars*
> *and watch (once again) the Hunter chase the Bull*
> *and the Twins as they taunt the Lion*
>
> *If I knew a house to rest in*
> *it would be beside Adam's stream*
> *and in the morning the warmth of sun on slates*
> *would wake me*[13]

(Michael Motteram)

In this case the turning of the form relates to the turning of the day that the poem speaks about.

In ancient ritual, however, the form almost was the meaning – mantric repetition whereby states of ecstasy and vision were induced. For modern people it might well be a question whether such techniques which dull the consciousness are still appropriate.

Alliterative Verse

We turn now to more subtle regularities – in the sounding together of consonants, and in the stress: e.g. some lines in Anglo-Saxon from 'The Seafarer' –

> *bitre breostceore   yebiden haebbe*
> *yecunnad in ceole   cearselda fella,*
> *atol ytha gewealc   thaer mec oft bigeat*
> *neoro nihwaco   aet nacan stefnan*
> *thonne he be clifum cnossath   calde gethrungen.*[14]

This was the accepted form of poetry in early Northern Europe, the law being that there should be four stresses in each line, two in each half-line: e.g.

> *neoro nihwaco   aet nacan stefnan.*

The third stress was the key to the alliteration (i.e. the repetition of consonants) – in this case, 'nacan.' One of the first two stresses had to alliterate with it, both could if desired (they both do in this example). The fourth stress was not allowed to alliterate. The number of syllables between stresses varied considerably.

   Here is a translation which attempts to abide by those laws:

> *Breast-drought I have borne, and bitternesses too.*
> *I have coursed my keel through care-halls without end.*
> *Over furled foam, I forward in the bows*
> *Through the narrowing night, numb, watching*
> *For the cliffs we beat along ...*[15]

(trans. Michael Alexander)

Exercise 250
Write a few lines in Anglo-Saxon (even if you do not know any), obeying the rules of alliterative verse [see also *p. 183*]. Read them (one line each) round the group as a continuous poem.

Exercise 251
Try the same, using modern English words. It might be helpful to take storm or conflict as subject matter. If you wish to practise alliterating before relating it to stress patterns, turn back to *p. 113*.

   Alliterative verse (or any other form) should not be regarded as merely an outward literary device. It arose out of the temperament and environment of those early Norse people. We must imagine them around the hearth-fire in their great wooden halls, listening to the 'scop' as he recited the tribal stories. In pre-Christian times he would have sung of the first being, Ymir, who was created out of the meeting of fire and ice [see *p. 83*]. Such images are typical of these folk, who came to experience their very identify in the clashing of opposites – in the sword-fight (they even gave names to their swords), in the word-fight [see *p. 85*], in their strife with the elements at sea. Maybe those elements were beating against the walls as the poet told his story; but what they heard was more than wind and snow – it was the creative and destructive forces that were there 'in the beginning'. These elements were ensouled. 'Weird' was out there in the dark, weaving their destinies. The 'Un-things' were out there; and the poet, by naming the sources of Creation and binding their elemental power into his consonants, held boundaries against chaos.

With the coming of Christianity, and of writing, into England, and with the influx (after 1066 A.D.) of French words and sensibilities into the language, these verse forms began to lose their vigour. We still hear echoes of it in this lyric from the 15th century, (another example of a turning poem):

> *I sing of a maiden*
> *That is makeles:*
> *King of all Kings*
> *To her Son she ches.*
>
> *He cam also stille*
> *There his moder was*
> *As dewe in Aprille*
> *That falleth on the gras.*
>
> *He cam also stille*
> *To his modres bowe*
> *As dewe in Aprille*
> *That falleth on the flowr.*
>
> *He cam also stille*
> *There his moder lay*
> *As dewe in Aprille*
> *That falleth on the spray.*
>
> *Moder and maiden*
> *Was nevere noon but she:*
> *Wel may swich a lady*
> *Godes moder be.*[16]

But it is impossible to imagine the hero, Beowulf, singing like that to any Lady. Only when (through some vast inner shift) the vowels and rhythms of the language had become singable, could such subtleties of feeling come to expression.

Motion and Emotion

After some time together in the group it will be obvious that each person's written or spoken language has a distinct movement or rhythm, or lack of rhythm. How did those rhythms get there? It is a difficult question – as difficult as saying how we move our arms – the sources of will are so asleep in us.

One thing is certain: as human beings we are rhythmic beings. Countless rhythms are at work in us, by hour, week, month, season, year, breath. If those motions stopped we would stop, too. Perhaps only in our experience of 'I' does rhythm come to 'the still point of the turning world.' We all breathe, but we breathe differently. Some have a mighty bardic breath, while others sigh intimately. It shows in the way we speak, and in our writing.

When [*exercise 158*] we made new languages to embody the qualities of the four elements we saw that their movements (or tempos) corresponded to those of the human temperament. The temperament of a person or a nation can often be discerned in the rhythms of their language. It would be good to practise those tempos which you find most difficult.

Exercise 252
This can be carried over into pieces for the different animals. What we learned about the relationship of animals to human emotions [*p. 58*], and, now, about the movements of the different temperaments, could apply here. Consider, for instance, the different tempos of the Turtle and the Fish – e.g.

THE TURTLE

When Turtles dance with wrinkled feet
They do not move with every beat.
From side to side in ancient sway
One waltz can take perhaps two days.
They wait inside a sunbaked shell.
Lads or lasses – who can tell?

They never stomp on partner's toes
Except to wake them when they doze.
The bongo beat is much too fast.
They like a tune to last and last.
For Turtles dance with wrinkled feet
And do not move with every beat.

                                  (Michael Jacobs, Carla Mattioli)

THE FISH

Through the glass of a fishtank
Sunlight the warp
Water the weft

Threads of slender-spun gold
Weave in translucent tapistery
A single strand snaps

With the swish of a fish-tail
Light
Splits into shimmers.

                                                    (Carla Mattioli)

It may seem somewhat mechanical at first, but if you can give the attention and devotion to the task that Adam shows on the front cover of this book then life will flow into it.

Rhythm

Before we turn to work with strict metrical forms it is important to realize that rhythm is not the same as meter (measure), but is, in its essence, a flow in time, connected with the Greek goddess Rhea, whose name means 'flowing woman'. If that flow does result in a measurable form, it only proves that all forms in the world are mothered out of movement. To force language to conform to intellectual schemes imported from languages which have quite other rhythms can only be the death of poetry. When the heart is engaged, the movements of the language tend naturally towards a patterning.

The heart, it would seem, is the basis of the Greek epic line, the Hexameter: e.g.

$$-\cup\cup/-\cup\cup/-\cup\cup//-\cup\cup/-\cup\cup/-\cup\cup//$$

which corresponds to the human rhythm of four pulse beats to one breath. Thus in each line of the Hexameter (including pauses) we have two breaths and eight heartbeats. Only much later did the grammarians make an external measure of it.

Clearly there are jeopardies in the attempt to bring consciousness into this sleeping part of our nature, yet it is only by becoming conscious of any rhythmic difficulties that we might have, that we can begin to remedy them – not, at first, through language exercises, but by clapping, stamping, bouncing, skipping new life into our hands and feet.

Exercise 253
Stand in a circle and clap, each in turn, keeping to the interval of time established by the first two. Work until it is perfect.

Exercise 254
Now, with the feet – each person stamps in turn, *short/long*, right foot to left foot, again maintaining the established rhythm. Or the short can be by one person, the long by the next.

Once you have the idea you can devise your own rhythms. It may start as a mechanical metronome beat, but if you listen for what happens in between, then gradually you will feel that Rhea herself is present, something of her substance flowing between you. You probably remember games, such as Hopscotch, from your childhood; or Sevenses, in which a ball is bounced in rhythm. In this context you can revive them.

Exercise 255
Leading this back now to language, you can work further with counting-out rhymes [see *exercise 162*], or with skipping rhymes that you remember.

Exercise 256
Facing a partner, try the following sequence:

Slap your thighs/clap own hands/clap partner's hands/clap own/clap right hands/clap own/clap left hands/ repeat.

Then add this verse to it:

> *Im pom pe*
> *Polonee polonaski*
> *Im pom pe*
> *Polonee*

Academie Sofari
Academie puff puff.

It is no use doing such exercises just once. To become faculties they
should be practised regularly (you probably know others).

Meter

The many poetic meters were categorized by the early Greek
grammarians and eventually taken to be poetic law, but how useful
they actually are to the poet is uncertain.

The basic qualities that they embody polarize into falling rhythm
and rising rhythm.

Falling Rhythm (Thesis = foot down) comes to expression in the
Trochee –∪   e.g.

   Tyger, tyger, burning bright.

and the dactyl –∪∪   e.g.

   Don't be afraid of the voice of the thunderclap.

This is experienced as an initial movement which is then pulled back
and reflected upon. It is the Apollonian, thoughtful pole. It is the basis
of the Greek Epic poetry.

Rising Rhythm (Arsis = raising of foot) comes to expression in the
Iambus ∪–   e.g.

   I saw a peacock with a fiery tail.

and the anapaest ∪∪–   e.g.

   I agree that the green of the grass is a grace.

This is experienced as an ongoing progressive movement. It is the
Dionysian, wilful pole, and it was the basis of Greek Drama.

Exercise 257
Write one line in imitation of each of these basic meters. Explore
whether they do in fact have different qualities.

Between these two poles lies the Lyric of feeling. Some other basic
meters are:

   – –   Spondee   –∪–   Amphimacer

∪∪	Pyric	∪–∪	Amphibrachus
∪∪∪	Tribach	∪∪∪–	Paeon
– – –	Molossus	–∪∪–	Choriambus

Certainly it is good practice to work within fixed metrical forms. They are the finger exercises of the craft which, once mastered, can be dropped into unconsciousness.

Many examples from nursery rhymes have already been given [*exercise 37* and *exercise 60*].

Exercise 258
Write another verse for this well-known rhyme:

> *Simple Simon went a fishing*
> *For to catch a whale.*
> *All the water he had got*
> *Was in his mother's pail.*

Start each verse with, 'Simple Simon': Read them round the group as a continuous poem. If any sound awkward try to discover why, and improve them. [see also Limerick and Clerihew, *p. 115*]

Exercise 259
Gradually you can move towards more complex and serious forms – e.g. in imitation of this verse by Thomas Carew:

> *Ask me no more where Jove bestowes*
> *When June is past, the fading rose,*
> *For in your beautie's orient deep*
> *These flowers as in their causes sleepe.*
> *Ask me no more* ...[17]

Or of this piece by William Blake:

> *Sound the flute,*
> *Now it's mute.*
> *Birds delight*
> *Day and night.*
> *Nightingale*
> *in the dale.*
> *Lark in Sky*
> *Merrily.*
> *Merrily, Merrily*
> *to welcome in the year.*[18]

This begins with the amphimacer (–∪–) and then breaks free at the end, the contrast enhancing our experience of the quality of the movement.

If you are really looking for a challenge you could attempt to write a Sonnet. This form is not really suitable for group work, but it could be prepared for in the group in the following way:

Exercise 260
Find a Shakespearean sonnet, and recite the last words of each line e.g.

sea	–	*power*	–	*plea*	–	*flower*
out	–	*days*	–	*stout*	–	*decays*
alack	–	*hid*	–	*back*	–	*forbid*
might			–	*bright*		

or a Petrachian sonnet: e.g.

spent	–	*wide*		*hide*	–	*bent*
present	–	*chide*		*deny'd*	–	*prevent*
	need	–	*best*	–	*state*	
	speed	–	*nest*	–	*wait*	

and then compose your own versions of such fourteen word sonnets.

Exercise 261
Make up a new fourteen line rhyme-scheme, striving for unity of mood between the words you choose.

Shelley, in his sonnet, 'Ozymandias', tried this pattern:

land	–	*stone*	–	*sand*	–	*frown*
command	–	*read*	–	*things*	–	*fed*
	appear	–	*kings*	–	*despair*	
	decay	–	*bare*	–	*away*	

Does it satisfy your ear? It is clear from this work that rhyme is a rhythmic device, setting up expectations to be fulfilled later.

Exercise 262
Give your composed sonnet scheme to someone and have them make a full sonnet out of it. The content could be complete nonsense, or with a unified mood, if complete sense is too much for you. This (which is known as 'Bout-rhymes') can be done with simpler forms, such as the Ballad – e.g.

Bird/King/Heard,Sing.

Many forms of the sonnet have been attempted, but the two mentioned above have emerged as the most powerful. What is the emotional impact of the two forms? What do they do to you?

Verse and Universe

Such self-contained forms, again, are not arbitrary. They are the product and revelation of an age sure of its hierarchies –the Earth at the centre, and the nine 'crystal spheres' of the planets turning around it. The word 'consideration' (meaning 'with the stars') beautifully embodies that world-view in which everything, including human thought and language, turned at one with the uni-verse.

As soon as human beings started to imagine the universe in a different way, however, the old forms of language began to break down as well. The old mothering meters were no longer fit instruments for a thinking which had emancipated itself from the Cosmos. The new thinking had quite another gesture – prose, meaning 'straight on'.

Prose

In the 17th century the English language entered a new phase of development through the founding of the Royal Society of Science.

Bishop Sprat, one of its members, recommended that the use of simile and metaphor should be banned from Society proceedings, suggesting instead a 'return back to primitive purity and shortness,' believing that to be the 'natural way of speaking'. He was, in fact, taking the highly questionable position that prose preceded poetry.[19] In any case, it was necessary to develop a language suited to clear reporting of scientific research, unclouded by personal feeling and poetic ambiguities – i.e. the pole of communication had to be emphasized at the expense of expression [see *p. 42*]. This is admirably exemplified in the writings of Michael Faraday: e.g.

The theory of definite electrolytical or electro-chemical action appears to me to touch immediately upon the absolute quantity of electricity or electric power belonging to different bodies. It is impossible, perhaps, to speak on this point without committing oneself beyond what present facts will sustain; and yet it is equally impossible, and perhaps would be impolitic, not to reason upon the subject. Although we know nothing of what an atom is, yet we cannot resist forming some idea of a small particle which represents it to the mind; and though we are in equal, if not greater, ignorance of electricity, so as to be unable to say whether it is a particular matter or matters, or mere motion of ordinary matter, or some third kind of power or agent, yet there is an immensity of facts which justify us in believing that the atoms of matter are in some way endowed or associated with electrical powers, to which they owe their most striking qualities, and amongst them their mutual chemical affinity.[20]

The transparency and self-sacrifice of such language has to be acknowledged as a major achievement of scientific materialism. Concentrating, as it does, upon the content of what is said it is (unlike poetry) translatable into other languages.

Still more recently the terms 'prose' and 'poetry' have broken free from any formal classification. Poetry is no longer defined as something that rhymes and goes tum-ti-tum-tum. We speak today of free verse, rhyming prose, prose-poetry, so to explore the difference between 'poetry' and 'prose' becomes an interesting work:

Exercise 263
Write down two lines of poetry that have moved you: e.g.

> *I shot an arrow in the air;*
> *It fell to earth, I know not where.*

Are you sure it is poetry? Why? Would it still be poetry if it read – *I shot an arrow in the air, but I don't know where it came down?*

Exercise 264
Write a piece of prose on a given subject, and then a piece which goes towards the poetic: e.g.

> PLACE

In my opinion the best place in the world is to be found at the top of the bluebell wood. There is a little wooden stile there. Climb over it and you will find the place I mean. There is a log to sit on, and a furrowed field in front of you.

> *Some places are not places.*
> *This place is, though –*
> *this bluebell wood,*
> *this place where the world gathers,*
> *where the furrows of the field*
> *break wave*
> *upon wave against you.*

Of course, the 'poetic' piece will not necessarily be the better one or the more honest. That which was written as prose may well contain the real poetry, whereas the other may be full of tricks and devices. In which mode do you feel most at home?

Personal Style

Much of the joy of writing together in a group comes from the recognition of the great variety of ways in which people think and feel and (as an extension of that) use language.

Exercise 265
Write a paragraph on a given subject, then have a partner write the next paragraph in the same style – content, vocabulary, length and shape of sentences, should all be taken into account. More subtly, try to take on the movement and tone of the other person's voice. In the attempt you will also become aware of what it is in your own style that you have to sacrifice in order to enter faithfully into the other's.

Afterwards, the original writer can read out the whole piece, while the group listens for where the change came. It is more than a game, though. Style is (among other things) the expression of a person's unique being and, as such, needs to be approached with respect. The aim of the group is surely not to make everyone write like the teacher or like each other, but rather to permit that uniqueness to come to utterance.

Having said that, it is also obvious that we are in many ways trapped by our style; and so it is certainly part of the group's task to challenge mannerisms, conventions, slack rhythms, habitual vocabulary, verbosity, etc. Thus the group work becomes an exercise in self-knowledge as well as in language skills. The leader of the group has a responsibility here, recognizing the need to reach beyond empty word-play, and yet resisting the temptation to use the writing exercises for psychological manipulation.

Many influences come together in our styles of writing and speaking:

The spirit and conventions of our times:

We have been exploring something of this in recent pages. To make it conscious –

Exercise 266
Write a sentence, a line, a verse, a paragraph in the style of some well-known writer from the past.

Our sex:

Do women write differently from men? If you think they do, then is it because of convention? or different life-experience? or because of some fundamental difference between feminine and masculine psychology?

Exercise 267
This can be worked with by taking on fictional voices belonging to the opposite sex [see *p. 80*].

Our physical constitution:

The depth or shallowness of our breathing, the speed of our reactions, etc., surely influence the movement of our language. Working with the rhythmic exercises on *page 157* can make us conscious of this.

Our age:

Exercise 268
Write like a young child [see *exercise 55*].

Our temperament [see *p. 11*]:

Exercise 269
Bring the temperaments into dramatic dialogue.

Exercise 270
Or, bring the four kinds of sentence into dialogue. Some people are clearly exclaimers of life, while others are eternal questioners, commanders, or makers of wise statements.

Exercise 271
Enact a small scene and report on it through each of the four temperaments.
   Through such exercises you will become aware of the gifts and limitations of your own temperament.

Our soul configuration:

Another approach would be to observe whether your writing style is more nounal, adjectival or verbal, i.e. whether your thinking, feeling or willing faculty predominates. These, in turn, relate to the modes of epic, lyric and dramatic writing.

Exercise 272
Enact another scene, but this time have some members of the group write an epic (or narrative) response to it, some a more lyrical response, and some entering into the drama of the situation.
   In doing so you may, again, be forced to break out of your natural tendency. Although style *is* the person, it is also necessary in the craft of writing to have the freedom to take on the language suited to a particular situation or subject matter and, in the case of fictional dialogue, to find a voice belonging to the character [see *exercise 111*].

Our education:

Previous reading, personal memories, national culture, inhibitions placed on language through religion or upbringing ..... all these, and more, are the unfreedoms of style that we carry – and yet they are also our gifts, the particular instrument or per-sona that has been provided for our earthly journey.

Exercise 273

After you have become familiar with the characteristics of the styles present in the group, you can challenge each other by setting difficult tasks – the romantics to write without a trace of poetry or prettiness; the pragmatists to be utterly soulful, even sentimental; the describers to be reflective; the philosophers to be descriptive, etc.

In the end, though, our unique individuality is the author of our words, and even weaknesses and limitations are to be respected, for they are often the shadow sides of our strengths and potentials. The teacher needs to know this.

Exercise 274

Each write a few sentences, then gather them and have one person read them out. Can you guess who wrote which piece?

Sentenced by Sentences?

So far we have been working with the sentence as a closed form having a beginning, a middle, and an end in the best classical tradition. But must we really be sentenced by sentences in this way? Perhaps the real universe eludes us because of our insistence on experiencing it through such a form – gone before we have time to name it.

We have been looking here at ways of breaking free from those aspects of our personal style which fetter us; but since 1914 this throwing off of closed forms and creating in the face of the unknown has become a general endeavour of Western culture.

Exercise 275

Compose a fragmented page – e.g. page 127 of a mud-spattered novel found in the gutter, with words, phrases, whole sentences and paragraphs missing – the most exciting page. There is no need to know what belongs in the gaps, but work nonetheless out of a sense for the whole. In the reading let the silence be part of the expression, a stammering to communicate: e.g.

> .....*this house where love is stored.*
> *Her hair..............to surprise me............*
> .....*Fruit from the garden after a thunderstorm*
> ....*or found that suitcase*
> ....*old love-letters. 'Your white breasts'.....*
> ....*half-guilty, reading them......even the*
> *dead.....surprised in these dusty corridors.....*[21]

Or it could be a page from a letter, or from some ancient epic or scripture, 'torn into strips ... and stuffed into the mouths of mummified crocodiles', as were the poems of Sappho of Lesbos: e.g.

> *Pain penetrates*
>
> *Me drop*
> *by drop*
>   •
> *That was different*
>
> *My girlhood then*
> *was in full bloom*
> *and you-* [22]
>   (trans. Mary Bernard)

Exercise 276

Take a passage from a real newspaper or magazine and place into it similar creative gaps and silences; or fold one of the pages and read across to the next. What time and crocodiles accomplish elsewhere you can achieve consciously here.

The idea behind such Found Poetry is that the Muse not only drops words and ideas into our minds directly, but works externally, dropping poems and messages in the street if we have the eyes to find them and the nerve to claim them. Whatever the Self discovers uncovers the Self.

Chance

There are many instances in this book in which 'chance' is taken up into the creative process. Here are some others:

Exercise 277

Ask everyone to bring an object to the group in secret. Gradually bring them out and see what happens between them. Group them meaningfully. When they are all visible give someone the task to put them into an 'order'. [see *exercise 296*]

We can (in a Surrealist game known as 'The Exquisite Corpse') do the same with words:

Exercise 278

In a group (preferably five or more), ask the first person to write an adjective, the second a noun, the third a verb, the fourth an adjective, and the fifth a noun. In choosing them, feel that you are giving them as a gift for the group to work with. This is not to say that they must be 'nice' words, but words, nonetheless, that you can 'stand by' as you approach the jeopardy of the exercise. Write them in secret, then bring them together, word by word, into chance sentences: e.g.

dark	gipsy	learns	trapped	hazelnut
gnarled	clown	follows	misty	wardrobe
lucid	windows	fall	sleeping	eclipse
smiling	mountain	prays	sorrowful	saint

Usually when we come to writing we have our meanings already and choose words to express them, so it is good sometimes to free ourselves from that and let meanings arise out of the play of words. Sometimes, of course, there will be little interaction between the words, or the connections will be absurd and make you laugh. Sometimes marvellous half-meanings will shine through (often more satisfying than the explicit ones), or the sound or movement will satisfy you even though the sense is lacking. Observe your various responses.

We can take it further:

Exercise 279

Rearrange the words, within one line, or crossing between sentences. You can change the parts of speech, so that *misty* becomes *mist*, etc. In spite of the strict limitations you will find scope here for individual expression. Maybe in the whole history of the universe these words have never been together in the same sentence but have always wanted to be. Allow them: e.g.

dark	wardrobe	traps	fallen	saint
sleeping	clown	smiles	misty	hazelnut
dark	saint	prays	sorrowful	eclipse
smiling	gipsy	follows	dark	hazelnut
misty	smile	falls	dark	eclipse

Exercise 280

Work now with what lives between all the words, adding others as the need arises: e.g.

The Saint speaks: Asleep. Trapped in a dream. Fallen in a dark eclipse. Gnarled. Sorrowful. Praying for a window. It

will surely follow. The Smile. The mountain at the window.
Mist falling away. The mountain held in a hazelnut.

The Clown speaks: Trapped in a dark wardrobe. Eclipsed by
my own dark smile.

The Gipsy speaks: Nothing traps me. The mist is lucid. I follow
my own dark smile up the mountainside. I sleep by the falls.
The mountain is my window. The hazelnut is my wardrobe.

Exercise 281

This can also be done, conversationally, with a partner, each pair in the
group drawing upon the same pool of words: e.g.

What can you see out of the window?
Just mountains.
If I were a saint *I would live on a mountain like that.*
I can just imagine you praying there in the mist.
Outwardly misty, maybe, but lucid *inwardly.*
I'll stay here in the dark, *I think.*
Each has his path to follow.
Yes, and all are sorrowful.

Maybe, after all, it is not 'chance' we are working with, for according
to Carl Jung, everything that happens in the moment has the qualities
of the moment, and is related to us if we happen to be there and are
awake to it. For this reason Jung made a study of coincidences, or
'synchronicities' as he called them, concluding that in some cases they
were not random events, but events organized through laws other than
the cause and effect that we are usually aware of.[23] The artist can
participate in these laws:

Exercise 282

Each write one word on a small piece of paper, then pass it to the
person on your left. Now begin a piece of writing in which the word
you received is incorporated. When everyone is ready, pass on again
and incorporate the new word into the ongoing piece of writing. You
may not go back and change what you have already written. Seven or
eight words is usually enough to work with: e.g.

Please do not hesitate *to play the* violin *for me,* Sugar. Nobody
in the world makes me feel like you can. I will put on my lavender
perfume and you take off your rubberboots. *Afterwards we will*

dance *close together. And when the song has finished you will
whisper sweet lies in my ear.*   (S. Dagbjort)

There grew a lavender *bush in my garden.
Then somebody came with his* rubberboots
And danced *on its flowers,
Till it lay dead on the ground.
Without* hesitation *that somebody left
Leaving his* violin *on a purple bed.
A sweet taste of* sugar
For nobody *to taste.*

                                        (Franziska Friese)

This is an exercise in open form. You are in control of the writing, yet
at certain moments there are interventions from outside, moments of
'jeopardy' which need to be accepted as belonging to the event. Much
depends on your attitude. If you are not really in the moment the
things which belong to it will not declare themselves. It is possible to
carry such an attitude into your individual writing, allowing whatever
chances in your life to enter the poem.

Owen Barfield speaks of *a kind of thinking which is itself beyond words,
which precedes them, in the sense that ideas, words, sentences, propositions,
are only subsequently drawn out of it. This is that concrete thinking which is
the source of all such ideas and propositions, the source of all meaning
whatsoever. And it can only take the form of logical ideas and propositions
and grammatical sentences, at the expense of much of its original truth. For
to be logical is to make one little part of your meaning precise by excluding
all the other parts.* [24]

                                        (from *Romanticism Comes of Age*)

In these pages we are exploring those parts which are excluded through
our insistence on being logical.

The Stream of Consciousness

Exercise 283
Pick up your pen and write for seven minutes without punctuation and
without stopping: e.g.

> *This is a pen I'm writing with on a Thursday on a yellow paper
> without lines or fences the cows can get out and trample the*

golden corn the horses can gallop and flare their nostrils and race
all over the page and be foolish and wise at the same time and
not care that my pen can't keep up with them they are the
stallions whose manes flare back in the wind and in the north
wind and in the south and if I jump upon the word of a horse I
can gallop through dictionaries and diaries and bibles and put
my feet into stirrups made of gold and I can spur my horse faster
than a kangaroo who doesn't know his name oh dear this isn't
making sense I wish it was I wanted to impress the world with
my great writing but of course great great writing doesn't have to
make sense because sense is a fence that keeps the horses held in
their pastures snorting and champing I want a senseless horse to
ride who breaks all the grammars a slang horse an obscene horse
a horse that lies a horse that cannot distinguish nouns from verbs
this horse I love this horse is mine is me with black shining
shanks who knows where to go without whips and spurs what
his name is do I know don't I know unutterable dream horse
grammar book of the future.

This is an excellent task for those who are always judging their writing
while writing. Do not censor yourself or worry about bad grammar
(they do not have to be read out in the group). At moments of
blankness you can write 'blank', or whatever. You may find that the
writing flows at first and that after a while you panic; but keep writing –
it can be a creative chaos, and out the other side of it you can move into
a new world. On re-reading it note the different stages you went
through. Often (as in the example here) it becomes a writing about the
process. Such a stream of consciousness technique can help us move
beyond our usual reflective language into a language which partici-
pates in, and arises out of, the events of the world. Try to refrain from
revising them afterwards, for, as Jack Kerouac said, only first drafts
are preserved in eternity.

Exercise 284

Another way to enter this realm of language would be to write while
listening to music and to transcribe its movements and 'meanings' into
words and grammars.

A large part of this section has been given to the 'stream of the
antique song' (i.e. the poetic tradition) that Lorca acknowledges [*p.*
76] to be essential to the initiation of the poet. We have followed it,
somewhat chronologically, from magic charms, through alliterative

verse, metrical poetry, the development of prose, to surrealism and other modern experiments with form.

It is more than a history, however; it is an evolution, a movement of human consciousness which leaves its traces in literary forms and vocabularies showing very clearly (in condensed form) the transition from the language of *will* into a more *feeling* language and then into a language of the abstract *intellect*. [see *p. 139*] We have been following the English branch of the stream, being particularly (but not exclusively) concerned with the renewal of the English language. To impose old forms upon a modern consciousness (which stands constantly at the abyss of our imagined boundless universe) would be to hide ourselves from the Real. Yet, as Robert Duncan says, 'we have come so far that all the old stories whisper once more.' This stream from the past can help us to understand our present situation, and to bring new life to the 'Wasteland' that was experienced by so many 20th century poets.

Free Verse

It is not just a 'stream' that Lorca speaks of – there is also a 'fountain' of song, available to us at any moment. This, at its deepest level, is the meaning of 'free verse' – a new technique, certainly, but also a new way of experiencing the world. D. H. Lawrence called it the poetry of the immediate present, where the momentum of the moment fills our words:

> *In the immediate Present there is no perfection, no consumma-*
> *tion, nothing finished. The strands are all flying, quivering,*
> *intermingling with the web, the waters are shaking the moon.*
> *There is no round, consummate moon on the face of running*
> *water, nor on the face of the unfinished tide. There are no gems*
> *of the living plasm .... it is obvious that the poetry of the instant*
> *present cannot have the same body or the same motion as the*
> *poetry of before and after. It can never submit to the same*
> *conditions. It is never finished. There is no rhythm which*
> *returns upon itself, no serpent of eternity with its tail in its*
> *mouth.*[25]

The American poet, e.e. cummings, experimented a great deal with free verse forms: e.g.

no time ago
or else a life
walking in the dark
I met christ

jesus) my heart
flopped over
and lay still
while he passed (as

close as I'm to you
yes closer
made of nothing
except loneliness[26]

Test this by reading it aloud. Is it a chopped up piece of prose? Or does the breaking into line-lengths achieve something essential for the expression? Notice how, by isolating a phrase momentarily on a line, double-meanings are discovered – 'Jesus', becomes an exclamation as well as a name, and also becomes 'my heart.' The poem is set out on the page as a musical score, indicating how it should be spoken.

Exercise 285
Make some free verses of your own, using short lines [see *exercise 239*].

In free verse the line is as much a unit of breath as of meaning, continually taking hold of and releasing the breath of the one who reads or hears it: e.g.

THE THREAD

Something is very gently,
invisibly, silently,
pulling at me – a thread
or net of threads
finer than cobweb and as
elastic. I haven't tried
the strength of it. No barbed hook
pierced and tore me. Was it
not long ago this thread
began to draw near me? Or
way back? Was I
born with this knot about my
neck, a bridle? Not fear

but a stirring
of wonder makes me
catch my breath when I feel
the tug of it when I thought
it had loosened itself and gone.[27]

(Denise Levertov)

Whatever else this thread may be, it is the tug of the poetic line that she is on about – a verse about free verse, in fact, and good to practise on (how would you have shaped it on the page if had written it?).

This is not the rhythm of the old 'con-sidera-tions' [see *p. 161*] which so easily lull us or send us into ecstasy. Nor is it the movement of prose which has emancipated itself from hearts and stars. In free verse heart and head come together in a new relationship, its rhythms being created all the time at the edge of chaos, and we have to be wide awake to catch the meanings that are in formation there.

Six

The Hearth

STORY

To hold image, assonance, energy, apart in different sections of this book has been useful, no doubt, but in the end it is artificial. These fundamental aspects of language must flow together, beyond exercise and word-play, into fully articulated works – dramas, poems, novels, short-stories – the works of the future. That, however, is your task, for such longer forms are beyond the scope of this book, which has concerned itself with the craft and the inner faculties necessary for such a work. Anything beyond that must arise out of what you uniquely have to say.

In this final section we can take just one step towards such a synthesis by working with story, and in particular with fairy tale and myth. Arising, as they do, out of the oral tradition of the tribal or family hearth (before writing or television were invented) they lend themselves to the possibility of group work:

Exercise 286
If each person writes one word on a scrap of paper, folds it, throws it into the centre, and then takes another, you can spin a pen and the one it points to can begin to tell a story, incorporating the word that they received. After a sentence or two the next person in the circle can pick up the thread (the 'yarn') using their word, and so on, until all the words have been included. Afterwards the story can be re-told, even recreating it more fully.

The same can be done without any words being given.

It is important to carry a sense that you are not inventing the story, but that it is hovering in the room somewhere and hoping to be told now that its moment has come.

Robert Duncan says this:

> We all have a sense of the difference between what the story demands and what the teller of the story or the listener might like the story to be. The story that has been altered to be likely or true to some belief, or to be pleasing or to have some special effect upon its audience strays from itself. So too ..... in the light of the mythological, events and persons can seem true or false to the true story of who I am. [1]

(from *The Truth and Life of Myth*)

Exercise 287
Tell a spontaneous narrative to a partner. The partner may interrupt at

intervals with, 'No it didn't,' whereupon you must immediately change direction. After a few such interruptions you can say, 'Well, what did happen?, and change roles with your partner.

Out of such oral group exercises we can approach the writing of stories:

Turn again to the painting by Bosch at the beginning of this book. At first sight it seems to be a naturalistic scene, but look deeper and you feel yourself to be on the edge of a mystery, and that the central figure is not setting out on any ordinary journey, but upon the very 'path of the poets' that Lorca speaks of [*p. 76*]. That gate which is shaped so strangely opens upon the realms of fable, phantasy and fairy tale.

Fable

One way it opens is towards the animal fable, where the beasts are free to talk to each other out of the passions that they embody [see *p. 58*].

Exercise 288
Bring the animals in the painting into conversation – for example, the magpie at the gate with the magpie in the cage, or the swan on the Inn sign with the bird in the sky. The frozen moment of the picture is hereby brought into movement.

You could also bring the inanimate objects into dialogue – the slipper with the shoe, the knife with the spoon, the house with the tree, etc. Through such conversations the meaning and the details of the scene can be explored, even the 'moral', as Aesop and La Fontaine do in their Fables (try to find some examples).

Fable is a kind of riddle, really – the moral at the end being its answer. The parables of Jesus (though more subtle) are in a similar vein. Bosch's painting, in fact, is taken by some to be an illustration of the parable of the Prodigal Son.

[see *p. 81; exercise 74*]

Tall Stories

Another direction that Bosch's picture might suggest is the telling of boasting tales, tall stories, for this fellow crossing the yard is closely akin to the Fool who is number nothing in the Tarot Pack – trustworthy most of the time, but sometimes naught-y.

We have met such a character before in Nasruddin [*p. 94*]. We meet another in Baron Munchausen, Prince of Liars, whose fur coat (so he tells us), having been bitten by a rabid dog, proceeded to savage all the other clothes in his wardrobe. On another occasion, returning from a trip to the moon, he fell to the ground with such violence that he found himself in a pit nine fathoms deep. 'There was no other way than to go home for a spade and dig myself out by slopes.'[2]

Exercise 289
Write (in the first person) some of the tall stories that Bosch's (or anyone else's) character might tell as he wanders from pub to pub.
    [see *exercise 64; exercise 42*].

Gustave Doré: 'Baron Münchausen'.

Dream

More deeply, the gate of the painting is hinged upon the edge of sleep. It is not mere foolishness which makes this vagabond wear one of his nightshoes in the day time – it is the footwear of all poetic dreamers.

Exercise 290
Compose a dream narrative, starting from Bosch's picture if you want, or following where your own shoes lead you: e.g.

I am riding across a cold, windy field. It is not a man standing in front of me. It is a scarecrow. My horse shies in fear, and I have to use all my strength to hold on to her. This scarecrow is wearing one of my old jackets. Getting off my horse, I slip into the jacket and look at all the people around the table. It is Christmas 20 years ago, and the silver has been specially polished. How exciting to smell the candles and the Christmas tree! My sister leans towards me and hands me a small package. It is wrapped in paper made of a blue feeling, and I am a little frightened to open it. But I do open it, and in my hand I am holding an ice-horse, and a cold wind is blowing across the empty field.

(with Hans Peter Krieger)

Fairy Tale

Beyond even the dream, we come to the fairy tale where many such wise fools are to be found, princes disguised as paupers, magpies who are guardians of the path.

> *Why do you go so far from the little square?*
> *I go in search of magicians and princesses.*

(F. G. Lorca [see *p.76*])

We can accompany him on that journey:

Exercise 291
Take a walk with a partner, one blindfolded, the other leading the way and interpreting the landscape walked through (preferably a park or garden) in terms of a fairy story. People met by 'chance' can be incorporated into the event. Give a task (e.g. to bring back the flower that will heal the land). The one leading can also set trials and tasks. Upon return the one who was blindfold, and who heard the story, can re-tell it to the group.

> *Of all forms of literature, it seems to me, fairy tales give the truest picture of life. There may be errors in detail, but in a world so full of strange things they scarcely matter. Two-headed giants and beanstalks that climb up into the sky may not be true, but assuredly they are not too wonderful to be true. But the atmosphere of the fairy tale is astonishingly true to life. It deals*

*with the silent witchery that lies in common things, corn and
stones and apple trees and fire. It presents these, no doubt, as
magic stones and magic apple trees, and if anyone will stare at
them steadily in a field at twilight, he will find himself quite
unable to assert that they are not magic.*

*Let me take one quite practical example of the truth of fairy
tales. In these stories success is made to depend upon a number
of small material objects and observances; life is a chain of
talismans. If a man touches three trees in passing, he is safe; if
he touches four, he is ruined. If the hero meets a miller without a
beard, he is to answer none of his questions. If he plucks a red
flower in a particular meadow, he will have power over the
mighty kings of some distant city. Now this poetic sense of the
decisiveness of some flying detail is a thousand times more
genuine and practical than the pompous insistence on some
moral or scientific law which is the basis of most realistic novels.
None of us know when we have done something irrevocable.
Our fate has been often decided by the twist of a road or the
shape of a tree. Nay, it has often been decided by an omnibus or
an advertisement, and there can therefore be little reason for
denying that it is a magic omnibus or a magic advertisement.*[3]

(G.K. Chesterton, from The Ethics of Fairyland)

Yes, fairy tales have the power to awaken in us reverence for the magic
in everyday things.

If, while blindfolding our daytime eyes, we can keep inwardly alert,
visualizing the details of the story told by our partner and experiencing
the things of the world through it, we can start 'to open night's eye that
sleeps in what we know by day.'

Here are the opening paragraphs of three well known fairy tales, two
of them literary, one of them traditional. It is interesting to compare
the quality of the imagery and how the feeling is conveyed:

*"She said that she would dance with me if I brought her red roses," cried
the young Student; "but in my garden there is no red rose".*

*From her nest in the holm-oak tree the Nightingale heard him, and she
looked out through the leaves, and wondered.*

*"No red rose in all my garden!" he cried, and his beautiful eyes filled with
tears. "Ah, on what little things does happiness depend! I have read all that
the wise men have written, and all the secrets of philosophy are mine, yet for
want of a red rose is my life made wretched."*[4]

(from The Nightingale and the Rose, by Oscar Wilde)

*Far hence, in a country whither the swallows fly in our wintertime, there
dwelt a King who had eleven sons, and one daughter, the beautiful Elise.
The eleven brothers – they were princes – went to school with stars on their
breasts and swords by their sides; they wrote on golden tablets with diamond
pens, and could read either with a book or without one; in short, it was easy
to perceive that they were princes.* [5]

(from *The Wild Swans* by Hans Andersen)

*In olden times when wishing still helped one, there lived a king whose
daughters were all beautiful, but the youngest was so beautiful that the sun
itself, which has seen so much, was astonished whenever it shone in her face.
Close by the King's castle lay a dark forest, and under an old lime-tree in the
forest was a well, and when the day was very warm, the King's child went
out into the forest and sat down by the side of the cool fountain: and when she
was bored she took a golden ball, and threw it up on high and caught it; and
this ball was her favourite plaything.* [6]

(from *The Frog King*, by The Brothers Grimm)

It would be best to withhold the name of the author when comparing
them in the group. You can find other examples.

Exercise 292
Write your own first paragraph of a fairy tale, including a character, a
place and an action. Compare your results.

Exercise 293
Take one of the traditional fairy tales and, having studied it
beforehand, tell it round the group, each taking a passage and then
passing it on. Try, without being pedantic about it, to be faithful to the
details of the original. Comments during the process are not helpful.
Small mistakes and omissions can be left uncorrected unless, when
your turn comes, you can redeem them (mistakes can sometimes be
inspired re-creations). Such an exercise can help to develop the ability
to think in pictures.

Exercise 294
Write a fairy tale with a partner. If you do not have the time or patience
to write a whole one you could take the familiar theme of being lost in a
dark place, a forest, and groping your way towards the light – the door
of a house, perhaps, or a gate (some threshold inwardly seen). Go
through it, and describe what you discover.

   This task is a very difficult one for modern people. Apart from the
fact that castles and princesses no longer belong to our immediate

experience, our modern consciousness is one which separates meaning from image. Since Freud, Jung, and others did their pioneering work we know all the psychological interpretations of such 'symbols'. The traditional tales, however, emerged out of a consciousness which *thought* in pictures. Certainly those pictures are filled with wisdoms, but those wisdoms cannot be extracted from the image without reducing its meaning. The image is not the meaning in disguise – it is its revelation. So often, modern attempts at fairy- or phantasy-story make us feel that we are being preached at from beneath the surface.

> Goethe: *It makes a great difference whether the poet seeks the particular for the universal or beholds the universal in the particular. From the first procedure originates allegory, where the particular is considered only as an illustration, an example of the universal. The latter, however, is properly the nature of poetry; it expresses something particular without thinking of the universal or pointing to it. Whoever grasps this particular in a living way will simultaneously receive the universal too, without ever becoming aware of it, or realize it only later.*[7]

The feelings, too, are implicit within the things and events of such fairy tales, and are all the more moving for being unstated.

At first sight fairy tales seem to break all the laws of logic. On second sight it is clear that they have a logic of their own – not the laws of the physical world or of the abstract intellect, but of the soul. In this realm of play [see *p. 6*] and imagination, metamorphosis is the rule – frogs can quite lawfully change into princes. Further, though the progression of events and images does not accord with our usual ideas of cause and effect, it is nonetheless rhythmically ordered, appealing not to the brain but to the breath which understands such logic. Everything happens by number. To cross the *six* hills to where the *six* dwarves dwell would be an impossibility – it *feels* wrong, even if we cannot explain it.

This level of meaning in the fairy tale is ungraspable, however, without some sense of meaning in our own life-stories:

> *Do you go far, very far from the sea and the earth? ....I will go very far, farther than those hills, farther than the sea, close to the stars, to ask Christ the Lord to give me back my ancient soul of a child, mellowed with legends....*
>
> (F. G. Lorca [see *p.76*])

The fairy tale is there to remind us of our origins, and of the creative story that we belong to.

The Creation Story

Nu sculon herigean	*heofonrices weard*
Now we should praise	heaven Kingdom's guardian
Meotodes meahte	*ond his modgethanc*
The Creator's might	and his mindplan
Weorc Wuldofaeder,	*Swa he wundra gehwaes*
Work (of) Wonderfather	because he wonder of everything
ece Drihten	*or onstealde*
eternal overlord,	beginning established
He aerest sceop	*eothan bearum*
He first shaped	(for the) earth-sons
heofon to hrofe	*halig scypend*
heaven as roof	holy shaper
tha middangeard	*monncynnes weard*
then middle-earth	mankind's guardian
ece Drihten	*aefer teorde*
eternal Lord	after made
firum foldan	*Frea aelmihtig*
for men earth	God almighty[8]

This is the hymn to Creation that Caedmon composed in his sleep after leaving the hearthfire. It is translated here literally, word for word.

If Caedmon had lingered at the hearth he might possibly have heard the following passage from the great Anglo-Saxon epic, *Beowulf*:

> ....*Then the mighty spirit who dwelt in darkness angrily endured the torment of hearing each day high revel in the hall. There was the sound of the harp, the clear song of the minstrel. He who could tell of men's beginning from olden times spoke of how the Almighty wrought the world, a fair and bright plain which water encompasses; the victorious One established the brightness of sun and moon for a light to dwellers in the land, and adorned the face of the earth with branches and leaves; He also created life of all kinds which move and live. Thus the noble warriors lived in pleasure and plenty, until a fiend in hell*

began to contrive malice. The grim spirit was called Grendel, a
famous march stepper, who held the moors, the fen and the
fastness.....[9]

(trans. John R. Clark Hall)

Here we catch the poet at work, telling stories and, in particular, singing the Creation, much as Caedmon himself was asked to do.

It has been described already [*p. 154*] how the folk of the tribe must have experienced such moments – how wind and rain were ensouled for them, how the telling and riddling and bragging around the fire were an entertainment, yes, but one whereby the world and the kin were held together [see *p. 92*]. The poet, by the power of his word, held boundaries against the darkness.

But what story can the poet sing in our times? The rain is not ensouled for us, and it is impossible to sing that a Big Bang created us, or a chance conglomeration of dust and gases – there is no inwardness to *that* story. Every culture in history has felt the need to give some account of its imagined origins, and if our account is so empty of Being and creative activity then it tells as much about our present stage of consciousness, perhaps, as about the facts of world-creation.

Before the Beginning

What was it like before the world began? The ancient peoples never had to face such questions quite so nakedly. Their poets always stood between them and the Abyss, catching their hearts up into the tribal memory where they could share identity and origin with those dragon-slaying heroes – Beowulf, or Gilgamesh, or Michael, and beyond.

For us it is very different. In achieving an intense experience of our own unique individuality we have lost all memory of where we come from. We come from 'nothingness,' it seems.

That is where we should start, then –

Exercise 295
Define what it was like before the world began.

You could answer with more questions: e.g.

> *Was it dark? Was it still?*
> *Who was there? Who wasn't?*
> *Where were our faces?*
> *Where was it? Was there*

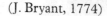

(J. Bryant, 1774)

> *a where there? Why?*
> *Who was there to ask it?*
> *Would the ear ask it?*

The task is impossible because

> *Who why where what when*
> *were not the questions then,*
> *they were the answers.*

because in trying to describe a state where opposites are united we are forced to use a language suited to a divided world.

Impossible, but do it anyway: e.g.

> *There were no secrets to be kept. No place to keep them. None to lift a finger to her lips to ssshh no noise. Only the hush of nothing rushed there between. Between was all there is. If was almost.*

As soon as you start using language to describe it you discover what an interesting kind of nothingness it is, full of exciting grammars – words take on multiple meanings, their own forgotten grammars wake up, parts of speech refuse to stand still, the tenses mingle.

However remote this may sound to you at first it is really not so, for often at the beginning of a group's working together this archetype of a space or chaos before Creation will arise spontaneously in the writing. It is the dark forest of the fairytale before the little house is discovered. It is a space for listening (necessary in all group work), a place of the breath held back, and containing the question, 'Who are you?' and 'Do we dare to share language together?' Ideally, between every question and its answer such a 'nothingness' will be present. It is the ultimate exercise of the 'negative capability' [see *p. 60*] that has featured so strongly in our work together.

In the Beginning

How did the world begin? There are many ways to approach this question:

Exercise 296
Each bring one object to the group in secret. Clear a space on the floor or table – a void suitable to receive a world – and begin to bring out the objects one by one, as intuition directs. Place them (physically, but

also through speaking) in relation to each other, creating a linked narrative about how the world began. Through imaginative naming seemingly unlikely objects can be included. Each act and word should be part of the event – no extraneous comments during the process; reflect on it afterwards.

Exercise 297

Or take the theme as a group exercise, combining speaking and writing [as described in *exercise 120*]. In the Hebrew story of Creation the Elohim (a plural noun) creates (a singular verb) the world. The plural acts singly – it is the ideal of all collaborative working.

Exercise 298

In the context of the present question, turn again to the conversation between opposites [*exercise 127*] – e.g. between dark and light, or form and energy, and have them declare their part in the world's creation.

This theme of the dynamic between polarities is present in any creative act. Often when a poem is on the way an inner tension arises between the absolute necessity to speak and the impossibility of doing so. Look at Bosch's traveller again – rich above, ragged below; his feet moving one way, his eyes turn another; he wears his daytime and his night-time shoes simultaneously; houseless, he is at home in every moment. Out of such inner tensions poems and worlds are created.

Exercise 299

> *SING THE CREATION:*
> *In the beginning, before there was light,*
> *there was a waiting eyesight,*
> *caught in the mind of God.*
> *It was the God before God.*
> *It was the mind before it minded.*
> *Slipshod, chaotic, it didn't care*
> *if anything got born or not.*
> *But the eyesight knew what it wanted....*
> *and a visible thing spilled out. It was*
> *an acorn*
> *bathed with eyesight.*
> *It started to roll.*
> *It reached the abyss of itself*
> *and fell plop! watersplash!*

into an ocean;
The eyesight warmed it. The water reached into it
and it burst forth into branches.
A branch must expect a bird.
So the eyesight flickered – once, twice.
It lidded the light. It lent eyes to the peacock.
She fanned the light into the folds of the waves,
and the goldfish flimmered.
Her piercing cry went rushing along the horizon,
curling and searching.
And infinitely far away on an empty beach
a listening shell woke up
and stretched a tender horn into the morning.
But the peacock's cry was lonely.
It cut day from night, sea from sky, shell from sand,
But could find no heart to understand.
Her thousand eyes shimmered.
Peacock longing bounded across the waves
where I in my small boat was paddling, idle.
I watched a snail crawl over an oakleaf.
I loved its trail of silver.
It drew my heart along.
Peacock cries passed me by.
Peacock eyes asked me nothing.

(with Cara Sullivan)

Another aspect of this theme concerns the origins of small particulars. Rudyard Kipling in his *Just So Stories* took up such questions as 'How the Leopard got his Spots,' in a somewhat playful fashion.[10] In earlier cultures it was a far more serious matter. Just as telling the Creation story was a ritual which held society together, so, in smaller things, by naming the origin of iron you could heal any wound that it gave you.[11]

Exercise 300

What is the origin of fire/iron/lions/daisies, etc.?

Do not be too ready to dismiss this as an outdated superstition. If, in our Western culture, we continue to see a tree, for instance as 'only a green thing that stands in the way,' and forget all gratitude and reverence for its creation, then our world, too, is in danger of losing its eco-logos. Through this exercise of imagining back into the origin of natural objects, or of our household things, we can bring healing to our un-whole-some ways of thinking which are laying the land waste.

It should be obvious that we are concerned here with the origin of meaning, and not just material beginnings. In which case, only you can answer whether these stories are true or not. Are you, in the moment of writing, being true to yourself? Does it feel right?

> John Keats: *I am certain of nothing but of the holiness of the Heart's affections and the truth of Imagination – What the imagination seizes as Beauty must be truth.* [12]

(from a letter)

The Act of Creation

The old storytellers had a repertoire for all occasions. Important human events – birth, marriage, death, the start of a journey – were, through the telling of the appropriate myth or legend, lifted into relation with their divine meanings and archetypes and given blessing.

The fact that such traditional forms no longer sustain us is not entirely a loss, though, for the nothingness in which we find ourselves is actually the price we have had to pay for our creative freedom. The poet H. D. (Hilda Doolittle) tells how, during the air-raids in London that were destroying the world she knew, the vision of a Lady was granted to her:

> .....*but she wasn't hieratic, she wasn't frozen,*
> *she wasn't very tall;*
>
> *she carries a book but it is not*
> *the tome of the ancient wisdom,*
>
> *the pages, I imagine, are the blank pages*
> *of the unwritten volume of the new* ... [13] ...

(from *War Trilogy*)

Starting, then, with a blank page in front of us, the creative act can be approached through four recognizable stages:

1. Writing about a subject matter as a detached (non-participating) observer. This is the pole of communication, language as a vehicle for clarity of thought (science, law, examination writing, literary criticism, etc.) – our whole civilization is founded upon it. Certainly it is to be respected; and if you need to work at it you should turn to the

conventional textbooks on how to write good English.

2. Seeing images inwardly while writing. As soon as this level is engaged the language becomes warmer. You can know that it is present when people start looking around the room or gazing into space to find the word they need. We can call it the level of **imagination**.

3. A state in which we listen for the next word, the whole body, even, becoming tuned for it. At this stage people often start using their hands to weigh the fitness of a word. Our ears as well as our brains begin to participate in the whole field of· meanings. This has to do with **inspiration**.

4. It is particularly in working with questions of Origin that a further level of the creative process opens. Here, momentarily, the gap between the form and the meaning is overcome; whatever information the language carries is experienced co-incidentally as a substance in formation – here we are creating a world as well as writing about one.

The mystic leaves language behind in the face of such ultimate questions. Poets somehow have to take language with them into the Wordless, and in doing so the act of writing itself becomes a contemplation out of which all language and grammars are re-created. In confronting a piece created out of this **intuitional** level we feel the absolute wholeness and necessity of its form. We no longer feel, 'I wish I had written that.' We feel that it speaks with our own voice, and we are healed by it.

N.B. The progression recognized here has a strong relationship to the progression through the various sections of this book.

The Four Elements

At the time of the transition from the old mythological consciousness towards our more abstract mode of thinking, the Greek philosophers were forever arguing as to which of these elements came first – choosing according to temperament, no doubt (and you can examine your own stories from that viewpoint).

The English Romantic poets, too, filled their poetry with such images – Coleridge with his sacred river, Alph, bursting out of the ground; Shelley with his 'Wild West Wind;' Blake with his burning 'Tyger' – as though the shaping forces of the elements, held in check by the Age of Reason, were straining to be released into renewed creative activity.

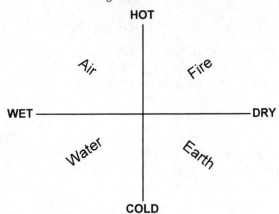

It seems that whenever we stand in the presence of a creative possibility these four helpers make their appearance. Earlier, [*p. 15*] we took a created object, a thistle, (i.e. something in its finished earthy state) and led it back through water and air into its fiery source (the same could be done for a human-made thing, such as a fairytale or a painting). And out of that experience we can certainly accompany Rudolf Steiner when he speaks of a universal creative process whereby from fiery enthusiasm, to air, to water, to our present earthy stage we have been measured into existence. Finished. Except that at this extremity we receive from the beings who created us fire in our thinking to be ourselves creators. It is a process we experience every time in our own creative moments – a spark received, then worked upon, fleshed out and brought into its final earthy form, but with a fiery seed within to kindle others.[14]

Throughout this book these four elements have been suggested as fit subject matter for the exercise of creative writing. Hovering as they do between the created and the uncreated state (neither too abstract, nor too particular), they declare the nature and the quality of the language we might use in praise of them. We write them even as we write about them, binding their living substance into the syntax.

What is scattered throughout the book can be briefly gathered here:

Exercise 301
Write a poem in a new language which expresses, even becomes, the qualities of a particular element [see *exercise 158*].

Exercise 302
Use real English words now for the same exercise, but use them for

their sounds and rhythms, not yet about the subject matter [see *exercise 168*].

Exercise 303
Lead it now into meaningful English, referring to the elements, suiting sound, rhythm, length and type of sentence, etc., to the subject matter: e.g.

> CHRYSOFAX
>
> *Being of light caught and held in my hand*
> *Hints of gold and amethyst*
> *   Striations out-of-true.*
> *A crystal cube, caught and skewed,*
> *A diamond, adamantine jewel,*
> *   Cut and carved in liquid darkness*
> *   Spun and spewed at the world's beginning*
> *Falling into my hand,*
> *Into a shaft of afternoon light*
> *Casting rainbows of splintered reason.*
> *O tethered piece of time, measured motion,*
> *   How can heart bear the silence*
> *   In this fragment of the uncreated light.*

(Cara Sullivan)

Exercise 304
Address the elements as beings [see *p. 107*]. Praise them. Invoke their powers and graces.

Exercise 305
Enter into the elements now, and speak for them: e.g.

> *Fire, who are you?*
> *My red tongue lolls in the hollow log*
> *Licking and spitting*
> *Crowned with sparks*
> *And glittering stars.*
> *I'm the first risk of the fox;*
> *Fierce runs my light through his fur.*

Leave out the question at the beginning, add 'Who are you' at the end, and it becomes a riddle.

Exercise 306
Bring the elements into dialogue with each other (this might have already occurred in the conversations between opposites, *exercise 127* and *exercise 298*).

Exercise 307
Bring them into dialogue with a human being.

In this way, step by step – from 'it' to 'you' to 'I' – we overcome our usual onlooker stance towards creation and become participators in creative forces and with creative beings.

Ending Where We Began

Earlier [*p. 142*] we tried to find gestures expressive of command, exclamation, question, statement (the four elements as they appear in grammar). But if we look again at the picture of Adam on the front cover, which gesture do we see there? – all four together, and something prior to each of them, as he lifts his hand and listens inwardly to the Word from which all our earthly words and sentences draw their substance.

That was 'in the beginning'; but if this book has anything at all to say it is that this 'beginning' (in spite of all the noise and verbiage which tries to drown it out) is a potential within each of us. Caedmon, who least expected it, heard the still small voice of its angel. [see *p. 3*] And Hilda Doolittle, 'when the shingles hissed in the rain of incendiary', was covered by its wing, [see *p. 188*] finding a renewal there of her creative sources:

> ... *other values were revealed to us,*
>
>> *other standards hallowed us,*
>> *strange texture, a wing covered us,*
>
>> *and though there was roar and whirr in the high air,*
>> *there was a Voice louder,*
>
>> *though its speech was lower*
>> *than a whisper. ...*[15]

It is a voice which speaks, no doubt, differently in each person, yet if it speaks one urgent thing to us all it is the Word that we began with:

SING ME THE CREATION.

The Quintessence

Here, gathered back into the seed, is all that we have worked with. At the centre stands the 'I am', the primal sentence (logos) which contains all possible grammars within it. It is both subject (inner) and object (outer); both noun (form) and verb (movement). It is the four sentence types folded in one. All names and grammars that we know have fallen from that source, but through activating the 'I am' within us their given elemental powers can be worked through and filled with the ideals here inscribed around it.

N.B. A seed is not a summary; it is a fire placed under the earth to bring things into motion. So it can be left to you to quicken it by exploring what qualities and acts of language arise when these elemental powers decide to collaborate –

i.e. when Statement and Question listen to each other.

when Question and Exclamation wonder about each other.

when Exclamation and Command are moved by one another.

when Command and Statement give ground to each other.

when Question and Command wish each other well.

when Statement and Exclamation partake of each other's qualities.

Much of this is embodied (in a more artistic form) in William Blake's painting of Adam, where we see the earthly image of the 'I am' forming and informing, moving and being moved, in the overlap between inner and outer where living language arises.

Bibliography

Section 1

1. The Venerable Bede, *Ecclesiastical History.*
2. *The Gospel According to St. Matthew,* Ch.10, V.35, Authorised Version.
3. *The Earliest English Poems,* trans. Michael Alexander, Penguin Books, Harmondsworth, 1966, p38.
4. W.B. Yeats, *The Collected Poems of W.B. Yeats,* Macmillan & Co. Ltd., 1961. p391.
5. Friedrich Schiller, *On the Aesthetic Education of Man,* Fredrick Ungar Publishing Co., New York, 1965, letter 15.
6. *Hymn of Jesus,* The Theosophical Publishing Soc., 1907, p37.
7. Rudolf Steiner, *The Four Temperaments,* trans. Frances E. Dawson, Anthroposophic Press Inc., New York, 1968.
8. Margaret Colquhoun, director of the *Life Science Seminar* based near Edinburgh.
9. Karl König, *The First Three Years of the Child,* Floris Books, Edinburgh, 1984.

Section 2

1. *Genesis* Ch.1, V.1 , Authorized Version.
2. *Genesis* Ch.2, V.19, Authorized Version.
3. R. M. Rilke, *The Duino Elegies,* trans. J. B. Leishman and Stephen Spender, Chatto and Windus, London, 1977, p85.
4. Percy Bysshe Shelley, *A Defence of Poetry,* written 1821, published 1840.
5. From *Mid-Century French Poets,* ed. and trans. Wallace Fowlie, Grove Press, New York, 1955, p121.
6. Basho, from the translator's introduction to *The Narrow Road to the Deep North,* trans. Nobuyuki Yuasa, Penguin Books, Harmondsworth, 1966, p33.
7. Ibid, p32.

8. Ezra Pound, *Literary Essays of Ezra Pound*, Faber and Faber Ltd., London, 1960, p4.
9. Paul Matthews, *A Web of Birdsong Twisted*, Share Publications, 1976.
10. Sei Shonagon, *The Pillow Book of Sei Shonagon*, trans. Ivan Morris, Penguin Books, Harmondsworth, 1967, p170.
11. William Wordsworth, *Lyrical Ballads*, Oxford University Press, London, 1952, p246.
12. Paul Matthews, *Two Stones, One Bird*, Smith Doorstop Books, Huddersfield, 1988.
13. Paul Matthews, *The Fabulous Names of Things*, Emerson College, Forest Row, 1984.
14. Kenneth Clark, *Landscape into Art*, Penguin Books, Harmondsworth, 1956, p59, quoting from Leonardo's 'Treatise on Painting'.
15. Aylwyn and Brinley Rees, *Celtic Heritage*, Thames and Hudson, London, 1978, p319.
16. Lao Tze, *Tao Te Ching*.
17. Robert Duncan, *Roots and Branches*, Charles Scribner's Sons, New York, 1964, p30.
18. Samuel Taylor Coleridge, *Poems of Samuel Taylor Coleridge*, Oxford University Press, London, 1958, p276.
19. *Ecclesiastes*, Ch.9, v11, Authorized Version.
20. George Orwell, *Shooting an Elephant and Other Essays*, Harcourt, Brace and World, Inc., 1953.
21. Charles Dickens, *Hard Times*, Collins, London and Glasgow, 1961, Ch.1.
22. *The Book of Job*, Ch.39 V.19, Authorized Version.
23. William Blake, *Complete Writings*, Oxford University Press, London, 1972, p793.
24. Bernadino de Sahaqun, *Florentine Codex, General History of the Things of New Spain*, trans. Charles Dibble and Arthur J. O. Sullivan, University of Utah Press. Quoted in *Technicians of the Sacred*, ed. Jerome Rothenberg, Anchor Books, New York, 1969, p22.
25. Ernest Fenollosa, *The Chinese Written Character as a Medium for Poetry*, City Lights Books, San Francisco, p10.
26. Wallace Stevens, *Selected Poems of Wallace Stevens*, Faber and Faber, London, 1953, p43.
27. William Shakespeare, *Hamlet*, Act 3, Sc.2.

28. Charles Baudelaire, *Flowers of Evil*, trans. Wallace Fowlie, Bantam Books, New York, 1964, p27.
29. Edith Sitwell, *Selected Poems*, Macmillan, London, 1965, p34.
30. William Shakespeare, *A Midsummer Night's Dream*, Act 4, Sc. 1.
31. *The Song of Solomon*, Ch. 4, V.1, Authorized Version.
32. William Shakespeare, *Sonnet 130*.
33. From *Mid-Century French Poets*, ed. and trans. Wallace Fowlie, Grove Press, New York, 1955, p153.
34. Paul Matthews, *A Web of Birdsong Twisted*, Share Publications, 1976.
35. William Wordsworth, *Lyrical Ballads*, Oxford University Press, London, 1952, p232.
36. Apollinaire, *Selected Poems*, trans. Oliver Bernard, Penguin Books, Harmondsworth, 1965, p78.
37. Ralph Waldo Emerson, *Selected Prose and Poetry*, Holt, Rinehart and Winston, New York, 1962, p15.
38. Robert Graves, *The White Goddess*, Faber and Faber, London, 1977, p30.
39. *The Bhagavad Gita*, trans. Juan Mascaro, Penguin Books, Harmondsworth, 1973, p74.
40. Ezra Pound, *Selected Poems*, Faber and Faber, London, 1959, p129.
41. John Keats, *Letters of John Keats*, Oxford University Press, London, 1979, p43.
42. Ibid, p157.
43. Plato, *The Dialogues of Plato*, trans. B. Jowett, Random House, New York, 1937, p852.
44. Ibid, p865.
45. Hesiod, *Hesiod and Theognis*, trans. Dorothea Wende, Penguin Books, Harmondsworth, 1991, p23f.
46. Plato, *The Works of Plato, Vol. 1*, trans. Henry Cary, George Bell and Sons, London, 1907, p304.
47. Samuel Taylor Coleridge, *Biographia Literaria*, J.M. Dent and Co., London, 1906, Ch.14, p161.
48. Robert Duncan, *The Opening of the Field*, Grove Press, New York, 1960, p57.
49. *The Chatto Book of Nonsense Poetry*, Chatto and Windus, London, 1988, from 'The Hunting of the Snark', p297.
50. *The Epic of Gilgamesh*, trans. N. K. Sanders, Penguin Books, Harmondsworth, 1972, p70.

51. John Keats, *Letters of John Keats*, Oxford University Press, London, 1979, p157.

Section 3

1. Paul Matthews, *Verge*, Arc Publications, Todmorden, 1976.
2. Rainer Maria Rilke, *Letters to a Young Poet*, trans. as in *The Second Stage* by Betty Friedan, Michael Joseph, London, 1982.
3. William Blake, *Complete Writings*, Oxford University Press, London, 1972, p214.
4. *The New English Bible*, Oxford University Press and Cambridge University Press, 1970, p604.
5. *The Book of Enoch*, Ch. 41.
6. Francis Huxley, *The Way of the Sacred* (quoting Piaget's daughter,) Aldus Books, London, 1974, p68.
7. *Genesis*, Ch. 32, V. 24-32.
8. Federico Garcia Lorca, *Lorca*, trans. J.L. Gili, Penguin Books, Harmondsworth, 1960, p1ff.
9. Allen Ginsberg, Notes to *Howl and Other Poems*, Fantasy 7006, 1951.
10. (Source not traced)
11. Mark Twain, *The Adventures of Tom Sawyer*, Ch. 1.
12. Virgil, *Eclogues*, trans. E.V. Rieu, Penguin Books, Harmondsworth, 1972, p45.
13. Johan Huizinga, *Homo Ludens*, Beacon Press, Boston, 1955, p70.
14. *Beowulf*, (see note 16 for Section 6).
15. William Blake, *Complete Writings*, Oxford University Press, London, 1972, p149.
16. Rudolf Steiner, *Lucifer and Ahriman*, Steiner Book Centre, Inc., North Vancouver, 1976.
17. J.R.R. Tolkien, *The Hobbit*, Ballantine Books, New York, 1966, p86.
18. Iona and Peter Opie, *The Oxford Nursery Rhyme Book*, Clarendon Press, Oxford, 1967. Many of the Nursery Rhymes scattered throughout this book are to be found there.
19. Aristotle, *Aristotle's Poetics*, J.M. Dent & Sons Ltd., London, 1963, p38.
20. *The Elder Edda*, trans. Paul B. Taylor and W.H. Auden, Faber and Faber, London, 1973, p80.
21. Ibid., p14.

22. *The Earliest English Poems,* trans. Michael Alexander, Penguin Books, Harmondsworth, 1966, p101.
23. Idris Shah, *The Sufis,* W.H. Allen, London, 1964. p62.
24. Brih Upanishad, ii, 2, iv, 4., in editor's note from *Egyptian Myths and Mysteries* by Rudolf Steiner, Anthroposophic Press Inc., New York, 1971, p23.
25. *The I Ching, or Book of Changes,* trans. Richard Wilhelm, Routledge and Kegan Paul Ltd., London, 1965, p108.
26. Rudolf Steiner, *The Cycle of the Year,* Anthroposophic Press, Spring Valley, New York, 1984, p58ff.

Section 4

1. Samuel Taylor Coleridge, *Poems of Samuel Taylor Coleridge,* Oxford University Press, London, 1958, p288. ('The Ancient Mariner').
2. Rainer Maria Rilke, *The Duino Elegies,* trans. J.B. Leishman and Stephen Spender, Chatto & Windus, London, 1977, p87.
3. Rudolf Steiner, *Cosmic Memory,* Steinerbooks, New York, 1976, p72 leading to p81.
4. Dante, *The Inferno,* trans. John Ciardi, Mentor, New York, 1964, p160.
5. Source not traced.
6. J.R.R. Tolkien, *The Fellowship of the Ring,* Unwin, London, 1982, p311 and p332.
7. *The Dadaist Painters and Poets,* trans. Eugene Jolas, George Winterbourn Publishers, New York. Quoted in *Technicians of the Sacred,* ed. Jerome Rothenberg, Anchor Books, New York, 1969, p389.
8. Michael McClure, *Ghost Tantras,* distributed by City Lights Books, San Francisco, 1964, p46.
9. Mircea Eliade, *Shamanism: Archaic Techniques of Ecstasy,* Routledge and Kegan Paul, 1964.
10. Lewis Carroll, *Alice Through the Looking-Glass,* Macmillan, & Co. Ltd, New York, 1962, p20.
11. *Work Study,* XXC111, no 5, May 1953.
12. Thomas Carlyle, *English Critical Essays, (XIX century),* Oxford University Press, London, 1961, p221.
13. E. Clerihew Bentley, *The Complete Clerihews of E. Clerihew Bentley,* Oxford University Press, Oxford, 1981, p30.

14. G.M. Hopkins, *Poems of Gerard Manley Hopkins,* Oxford University Press, London, 1964, p70.
15. W. Nelson Francis, *The English Language, An Introduction,* English University Press, London, 1967, p1f.
16. Jean Piaget, *The Child's Conception of Life,* Paladin, St. Albans, 1977, p90.
17. Ralph Waldo Emerson, *Selected Prose and Poetry,* Holt, Rinehart and Winston, New York, 1962, p327.
18. Arthur Rimbaud, *Collected Poems,* trans. Oliver Bernard, Penguin Books, Harmondsworth, 1986, p12f.
19. Robert Duncan, *The Opening of the Field,* Grove Press, New York, 1960, p81.
20. Christopher Smart, *Jubilate Agno,* Rupert Hart-Davis, London, 1954, p106.
21. Rudolf Steiner, *Eurythmy as Visible Speech,* trans. V. and J. Compton-Burnett and S. and C. Dubrovik, Anthroposophical Publishing Co., London, 1956, ch.11, p18.
22. loc cit.
23. Rudolf Steiner, *Speech and Drama,* Anthroposophical Pub. Co., London, 1960, p378.
24. *Genesis,* Ch.11, V.1-9, Authorized Version.
25. Samuel Taylor Coleridge, *Poems of Samuel Taylor Coleridge,* Oxford University Press, London, 1958, p202. ('The Aeolian Harp')
26. Rainer Maria Rilke, a) *Selected Poems,* trans. C.F.McIntyre, University of California Press, Berkeley, 1964, p39; b) *Selected Poems,* trans J.B.Leishman, Penguin Books, Harmondsworth, 1963, p35; c) source untraced; d) *Twentieth Century Verse,* trans, Patrick Drinkwater, Penguin Books, Harmondsworth, 1963, p35; e) loc cit.
27. Edward Lear, *Nonsense Omnibus,* Frederick Warne and Co. Ltd., London and New York, 1943, p265.
28. William Shakespeare, *Sonnet 18.*
29. Arthur Rimbaud, *Collected Poems,* trans. Oliver Bernard, Penguin Books, Harmondsworth, 1986, p327.
30. Ibid, p171.
31. Allen Ginsberg, *Howl and Other Poems,* City Lights Books, San Francisco, 1963, p29.
32. John Masefield, *Collected Poems,* William Heinemann, Ltd., London, 1926, p56.

33. Gerard Manley Hopkins, *Poems of Gerard Manley Hopkins*, Oxford University Press, London, 1964, p70.

Section 5

1. *The Penguin Book of English Verse*, Penguin Books, Harmondsworth, 1963, p71.
2. T.S. Eliot, *Collected Poems 1909-1935*, Harcourt, Brace and World, Inc., New York, 1958, p70.
3. Rudolf Steiner, *Cosmic Memory*, Steinerbooks, New York, 1976, p51.
4. Federico Garcia Lorca, *Lorca*, trans. J.L. Gili, Penguin Books, Harmondsworth, 1960, p90.
5. Verrier Elwin, a reworking of his translation in *The Baigo*, John Murray, London, 1939.
6. Robert Duncan, *Caesar's Gate*, Sand Dollar, 1972.
7. Ernest Fenollosa, *The Chinese Written Character as a Medium for Poetry*, City Lights Books, San Francisco, p12.
8. *The Penguin Book of Chinese Verse*, trans. Robert Katewell and Norman L. Smith, Penguin Books, Harmondsworth, 1962, p7.
9. Christopher Logue, *Songs*, Hutchinson and Co., London, 1962, p76.
10. Samuel Taylor Coleridge, from a letter of Joseph Cottle.
11. *The Gospel According to St. John*, Ch. 1, V.1, Authorized Version.
12. T.S. Eliot, *Collected Poems 1909-1935*, Harcourt, Brace and World Inc., New York, 1958, p18.
13. *With My Heart in My Mouth*, (anthology) ed. Paul Matthews, Rudolf Steiner Press, Bristol, 1994.
14. from *The Exeter Book*.
15. *The Earliest English Poems*, trans. Michael Alexander, Penguin Books, Harmondsworth, 1966, p74. (Ezra Pound has also made a fine translation.)
16. *The Norton Anthology of English Literature Vol. 1*, W.W. Norton and Co., Inc., New York, 1962, p257.
17. *The Penguin Book of English Verse*, Penguin Books, Harmondsworth, 1963, p162.
18. William Blake, *Complete Writings*, Oxford University Press, 1972, p123.
19. Basil Willey, *The Seventeenth Century Background*, Chatto and Windus, London, 1962, p210ff (quoting *The History of the Royal Society*, by Thomas Sprat.)

20. J.G. Crowther, *British Scientists of the C19th*, Vol.1, Penguin Books, Harmondsworth, 1940, p128.
21. Paul Matthews, *Footnotes*, Writer's Forum, London, 1971, p51.
22. Sappho, *Sappho, A New Translation*, trans. Mary Barnard, University of California Press, Berkley and Los Angeles, 1962, fragments 61 and 68.
23. *I Ching, or Book of Changes*, Routledge and Kegan Paul Ltd., London, 1968 (see the Foreword by Carl Jung).
24. Owen Barfield, *Romanticism Comes of Age*, Rudolf Steiner Press, London, 1966, p77.
25. D.H. Lawrence, Preface to the American edition of *New Poems*, Viking Press.
26. e.e. cummings, *Selected Poems*, Penguin Books, Harmondsworth, 1960, p72.
27. Denise Levertov, *The Jacob's Ladder*, New Directions, New York, 1961, p48.

Section 6

1. Robert Duncan, *The Truth and Life of Myth*, The Sumac Press, Fremont, 1968, p7.
2. R.E. Raspe, *Baron Münchausen*, Dover Publications Inc., New York, 1960, p23.
3. G.K. Chesterton, *The Man Who Was Orthodox*, A.P. Watt and Son.
4. Oscar Wilde, *The Works of Oscar Wilde*, Collins, London and Glasgow, 1962, p262.
5. Hans Andersen, *The Wild Swans*, translation untraced.
6. The Brothers Grimm, *The Complete Grimm's Fairy Tales*, Routledge and Kegan Paul, London, 1975, p17.
7. J.W. von Goethe, (source not traced).
8. The Venerable Bede, *Sweet's Anglo-Saxon Reader*, ed. Whitelock, Clarendon Press, Oxford, 1970, p67.
9. *The Norton Anthology of English Literature*, Vol. 1, trans. R. Clark Hall, W.W. Norton and Co. Inc., New York, 1962, p32.
10. Rudyard Kipling, *Just So Stories*, Macmillan & Co. Ltd., London and Basingstoke, 1981, p43.
11. See Rune IX of the Finnish Epic, *Kalevala*, trans. W.F. Kirby, J.M. Dent and Sons Ltd., London, 1974, p78.
12. John Keats, *Letters of John Keats*, Oxford University Press, London, 1979, p36f.

13. H.D. (Hilda Doolittle), *Collected Poems 1912-1944*, New Directions, New York, 1983, p569f.
14. Rudolf Steiner, *Occult Science – an Outline*, trans. George and Mary Adams, 1963, Ch.4.
15. H.D. (Hilda Doolittle), *Collected Poems 1912-1944*, New Directions, New York, 1983, p520f.

N.B. Many of the examples for exercises arose out of group work, some collaboratively, some individually, and (wherever possible) the writers have been acknowledged. Some have appeared previously in a booklet entitled, *Poetry Around the Table*, produced by the Friends of the School for Speech Formation, at Peredur Centre for the Arts, East Grinstead. Some others are drawn from *Treetops*, a collection (unpublished) made by Barbara Hollander out of group work with the author. Experimental pieces by Paul Matthews are also included.

Other books available from Hawthorn Press

FESTIVALS TOGETHER
A guide to multi-cultural celebration.
Sue Fitzjohn, Minda Weston, Judy Large.
This is a resource guide for celebration, and for observing special days according to traditions based on many cultures. It brings together the experience, sharing and activities of individuals from a multi-faith community - Buddhist, Christian, Hindu, Jewish, Muslim and Sikh. It draws on backgrounds as diverse as north and west Africa, the Caribbean, China, India, Ireland, Japan, New England, the Philippines and more. Its unifying thread is our need for meaning, for continuity and for joy.

Festivals Together seeks to enrich and widen our celebration experience and to reflect the 'global village' nature of modern society. As a learning tool or 'just for fun', it offers a creative influence for children today.

Festivals Together is a resource guide which will be of use to every school and family. It has been written with teachers and parents in mind. Sue Fitzjohn is a primary school head and Minda Weston teaches in Widden School, Gloucester. Judy Large is an author of *Festivals, Family and Food.*

Richly illustrated, there is a four page insert of seasonal prints by John Gibbs for your wall.
200 x 250mm; 224pp; limp bound; colour cover; fully illustrated.
ISBN 1 869 890 46 9

THE LISTENING EAR
The development of speech as a creative influence in education.
Audrey E McAllen.
This book gives teachers an understanding of speech training through specially selected exercises. These aim to help develop clear speaking in the classroom and to assist those concerned with the creative powers of speech as a teaching tool. The author looks at the links between speech and child development, the speech organs, the effects of artificially produced sound on speech development, rhythm, metre and the sound groups.
210 x 135mm; 162pp; sewn limp bound; 36 illustrations.
ISBN 1 869 890 18 3

THE ORIGIN AND DEVELOPMENT OF LANGUAGE
Roy Wilkinson.
Many years of working as a Waldorf teacher enable the author to offer a wide-ranging survey of the origin of language. He traces language from its spiritual roots to the almost soulless polyglot that we call language today. He enthusiastically uncovers the many layers contained in the English language, and discusses how we can rediscover a true way of knowing how, and what, we speak.
216 x 138mm; 64pp; paperback.
ISBN 1 869 890 35 3

CREATIVE FORM DRAWING 1
Rudolf Kutzli.
297 x 210mm; 152pp; sewn limp bound.
ISBN 1 869 890 28 0

CREATIVE FORM DRAWING 2
Rudolf Kutzli.
297 x 210mm; 152pp; sewn limp bound.
ISBN 1 869 890 14 0

CREATIVE FORM DRAWING 3
Rudolf Kutzli. Translated by Roswitha Spence.
297 x 210mm; 152pp; sewn limp bound; fully illustrated.
ISBN 1 869 890 32 9

THE LADY AND THE UNICORN
Gottfried Büttner. Translated by Roland Everett.
All great works of art stimulate the observer to ask questions. Here the author discusses the symbolism and real significance of the beautiful but enigmatic tapestries of the Paris Cluny Museum. Every work of art is rooted in culture and history, and their interpretation can provide valuable insights into the universal nature of the human being.
297 x 210mm; 80pp; printed paper case hardback; colour cover; 16 colour plates.
ISBN 1 869 890 52 3

NEW EYES FOR PLANTS
A workbook for observing and drawing plants
Margaret Colquhoun and Axel Ewald

Here are fresh ways of seeing and understanding nature with a vivid journey through the seasons. Detailed facts are interwoven with artistic insights. Readers are helped by simple observation exercises, by inspiring illustrations which make a companion guide to plant growth around the year. This shows how science can be practised as an art, and how art can help science through using the holistic approach of Goethe. A wide variety of plants are beautifully drawn, from seed and bud to flower and fruit. The drawings are accompanied by helpful suggestions which encourage readers to try out the observation and drawing exercises. Dr Margaret Colquhoun researches into plants and land-scape. Axel Ewald is a sculptor. The book is the outcome of their teaching and research work.
270 x 210mm; 208pp; paperback; colour cover; black and white illustrations.
ISBN 1 869 890 85 X

SPEECH AND SPEAKING IN THE CLASSROOM
Roy Wilkinson

This practical guide for teachers shows how speech can be developed through creative classroom exercises.
216 x 138mm; 96pp.
ISBN 1 869 890 87 6

MORE PRECIOUS THAN LIGHT
How dialogue can transform relationships and build community
Margreet van den Brink

Profound changes are taking place as people awaken to the experience of the Christ in themselves. The author is a social consultant and counsellor and offers helpful insights into building relationships. She shows how true encounter can be fostered.
216 x 138mm; 160pp; colour cover.
ISBN 1 869 890 83 3

TROLL OF TREE HILL
Judy Large.   Illustrations by Tom Nelson
We have all heard about children who do not believe in fairies or trolls. Here is a story about a troll who does not believe in children. With his age-old hatred of humankind, how will Troll handle the sudden invasion of his woodland home? This old fashioned story book for children aged eight to one hundred and eight is beautifully illustrated with twenty eight full page line drawings by Tom Nelson.
210 x 297mm; 72pp; colour cover; illustrations; softback.
ISBN 1 869 890 74 4

THRESHOLDS
Near-life experiences
Edited by Gabriel Bradford Millar
People returning to life from serious accidents sometimes describe their near-death experiences. Such experiences may include brief glimpses of sustaining light, of healing, of helping beings, and often the painful realisation that it is not yet time to cross the threshold of death. Such breakthroughs into a different reality are also being experienced by people in everyday life situations. This book is a gathering of their accounts of their 'near-life' experiences, moments of openness, transformation or total clarity which become turning points.
216 x 138mm; 192pp; 4 colour cover; photos.
ISBN 1 869 890 68 X

If you have difficulty ordering from a bookshop, please order direct from:
Hawthorn Press,
Hawthorn House, 1 Lansdown Lane, Stroud, GL5 1BJ, UK
Telephone 01453 757040
Fax 01453 751138